With Christ *Today* in Paradise

With Christ *Today* in Paradise

KENNETH L. THRASHER

RESOURCE *Publications* · Eugene, Oregon

WITH CHRIST *TODAY* IN PARADISE

Resource Publications
A Division of Wipf and Stock Publishers
199 W. 8th Ave., Suite 3
Eugene, OR 97401
www.wipfandstock.com

ISBN 13: 978-1-49825-438-0

Manufactured in the U.S.A.

To my four excellent grandchildren who mean so much to me:
Russell Thrasher, Justin Thrasher,
Nina Becksted, and Nick Becksted.

Contents

Preface

THERE ARE MANY WORKS, both ancient and recent, which treat the same subject as my little book which you hold in your hand. That subject is attaining the higher spiritual life.

I am very glad that you have picked mine, which I consider to be unique, out of the great variety of writings now available on the subject. Let us believe that the Lord has led you to this act of choice! Let us affirm that the Lord has willed that you should consider what I have to say on this matter.

Writings like mine were sometimes called "A Method of Prayer" during the Middle Ages. The content of such a work was usually the presentation of a technique of spiritual advancement with the object of coming to God in a very special way; one much beyond the general religious impressions one receives in the ordinary Christian life. That is good company to be in. However, another category appeals to me as a descriptive classification of my work. By stretching the imagination, I might call it a Mystical Theology. Justification for this would include the fact that I treat many theological topics which function either as presuppositions of the transcendent experience I describe or are valid implications of that experience.

Neither a textbook nor a scholarly exposition of mysticism, my book is rather an account of my own personal mystical experience set in a theological framework. Exposition of Christ's promise to the convict who was dying on the next cross leads me to redefine transcendental experience as being with Christ in paradise. This I understand as an event of the soul which occurs when the normal psychic functions are over-ridden and a totally new and different spiritual state replaces them. This state consists of increasing degrees of ecstatic feelings of being incorporated into the heavenly glory and standing in the presence of God. Yet one does not visually behold God. The higher one rises in feeling toward the throne of grace, the more the divine splendor overwhelms the capacity of seeing Him who is, as the hymn writer said, "Pavillioned in splendor, and girded with praise."[1] That is, the divine attributes protect the divine person from our curiosity. This is the same device as described by Pseudo-Dionysius as "Divine Darkness,"[2] which results when the splendor of God prevents the vision of God.

The unique feature of my approach is the emphasis I place on the "ontological presence" of God as the constitutive ground of the soul. This leads me to expound the soul and its marvelous functions in lyrical terms and point to the "breath of God" or "the light that lights every man" as the *sine qua non* of our existence as human. As the breath of life or the light that lights every man makes us human, the indwelling Christ, activated by personal faith, makes us Christian.

While emphasizing that transcendent experience cannot be commanded at will, regardless of the intensity of the spiritual discipline or the fervency of our desire for it, several spiritual exercises are presented which help prepare us to hear and accept the invitation of God to enter paradise with Christ should it come to us. The Apostle Paul specifically interpreted his mystical elevation as being ". . . caught up into paradise,"[3] after which he resumed his historical existence.

All true religious experience is a gift of God's grace. He honors no technique which would presume to manipulate Him or subject Him to some strategy for coming into His presence. No mechanical devices will open the heavenly door to paradise. However, some system of devotion may be very helpful and enable us on some level of intensity, even if it does not open the gates to heaven, to "practice the presence of God,"[4] to use Brother Lawrence's famous term, thereby preparing us to accept the divine invitation if it should be issued.

While I recognize that the deeper religious experience, or, as I have called it, being with Christ in paradise, is really beyond our capacity to describe, I nevertheless want to present a capsule summary of my own.[5] First, there was a startling awakening resembling an abrupt strike on the

---

1. Robert Grant, "O Worship the King," *The Baptist Hymnal*, ed. Wesley L. Forbis (Nashville: Convention Press, 1991), 16.

2. Dionysius the Areopagite, *Mystical Theology*, ch.1, http://www.esoteric.msu.edu /VolumeII/MysticalTheology.html.

3. Second Corinthians 12:4a.

4. Brother Lawrence, *The Practice of the Presence of God: The Best Rule of Holy Life*, http://www.ccel.org/ccel/lawrence/practice.ii.html.

5. Kenneth L. Thrasher, *Jesus Christ Is With Us* Smithfield N.C: 1983. My first attempt to describe my religious experience is presented in this volume.

head, followed by an awareness of a warm brilliance in the region of my heart. Almost simultaneously, a "luminous pinpoint," a brilliant speck of light appeared, seemingly infinitely distant from me which began to move toward my "being," with increasing brightness, generating oceanic feelings in me accompanied by a very quiet ecstasy with no ordinary emotional accompaniment. Then it seemed to "break" into my being from below and began a steady upward climb through me, producing the most profound feelings of joy and praise. After a slow and deliberate ascent, it entered into what I called my "heart," joining the Holy Spirit which seemed to be awaiting its arrival. After this luminous pinpoint, which I later understood as the "ontological light" which forms the soul, united with the waiting Holy Spirit together they began an upward movement to a level which I later called "beyond the heart," to enter into eternal realms beyond the self, taking me into the heavenly realm with "them." *There*, I was enfolded and penetrated by Light, heard music, sang silent praises making not a single sound, basked in the divine presence, felt power, received grace, and accepted a call. Later, I designated this state as Light/joy, since the two were inseparable. As inadequate as that term is, it was the best I could do at the time. After reaching an apex of exhilaration and ecstatic feelings, while my consciousness continued to overflow with doxological affirmations and silent praise, a slow process of withdrawal began, consisting of undulating surges in which the peak became gradually lower on recurring upward movements. Finally, the withdrawal was complete and I was at perfect rest and peace, wholly integrated and feeling fantastically blessed and called to extraordinary service of God. A fuller exposition is contained in several chapters in the book.

Adequate description *is* beyond the reach and range of human language, or at least mine, as I have just demonstrated. Its essence cannot be captured in ordinary words. This must be why the practitioners of the "inward way" do not often attempt to communicate their deepest and highest experience. It just continues to elude our efforts to express it and our verbal presentations always fall short and leave us disappointed.

Also, telling about it seems to be a violation of spiritual privacy. Nevertheless, after many years I now offer my reflections to you in this form in the hope that they will prepare you for traversing the inward way to the presence of God and encourage you to seek this amazing blessing. I send this forth in an attitude of prayer with the highest hopes for your spiritual adventure.

Sincerely,
Kenneth L. Thrasher

1

The Promise of Paradise

JESUS SAID TO THE convicted criminal dying with Him on an adjacent cross, ". . . Verily I say unto thee, Today shalt thou be with me in paradise."[1] Although this promise was made privately and exclusively to the man indicated, it is implicit in the act of salvation and is therefore a promise to every Christian believer (except for the temporal qualification "To day"). The crucified thief must die in order to receive the promise but since both his death and the death of Christ were imminent, this posed no problem for him. Indeed, deliverance from the dire circumstances in which he found himself was a culmination much to be desired. So he died with Christ on Calvary. In fact, he alone among the sons of men died *twice* with Christ. He died with Him when he put his trust in Christ, reaching out to Him for salvation. The Apostle Paul interpreted the exercise of saving faith as dying spiritually with Christ, participating in His death and subsequent resurrection.[2] In addition to entering into the death of Christ spiritually in advance, he also actually and literally died with Christ. Both he and Christ died that day. And the promise to him was fulfilled then and there.

We who have spiritually died with Christ through faith, entering into His death, also are heirs of the promise: "You shall be with me in paradise." It is contained in our salvation. The exception is that "today" is not an essential dimension of the promise to us. Someday, we shall be with Him in paradise in the absolute sense, but probably not today. God grants us time and space in which to continue our lives, to realize our calling and destiny,

1. The Holy Bible (Cambridge: Printed at the University Press, London & New York) Luke 23:43. All Biblical references are from this King James Version unless otherwise indicated.

2. Romans 6:1–11.

to continue to live and move and have our being both in Christ and in the earthly sphere as we continue our historical existence.

Yet it is possible or even probable that some who are reading this now will in fact be with Christ in paradise today in the final sense, that is, through the experience of death. We must all pass through death to receive the promise *literally* and enter into that permanent state of bliss with Christ in the heavenly realm, the exception being those who are still alive at the second coming of Christ (the *parousia*).[3] Meanwhile, we rejoice because God has given us time and space in which to realize our destiny and calling.

But there is a real sense in which we can enter into paradise with Christ and at the same time continue our earthly, historical existence. In this sense the *today* of Christ's promise to the thief on the cross may apply to us also. However, we must broaden our understanding of the term "being in paradise with Christ." Paul the Apostle explicitly claims to have been "caught up into paradise" and "caught up into the third heaven."[4] Paul is describing a state of his soul in which he was elevated to unearthly heights, taken into glory, stood before the Lord, and heard words that could not be uttered by human tongue.

On that day Paul was in paradise with Christ, yet he continued to live and, although uncertain as to whether he was "in the body or out of the body," to exist in the earthly, historical realm while the experience was occurring. So for Paul, "being with Christ in paradise" in the here and now is a spiritual event in which the soul by its marvelous capacities granted to it in creation, apprehends and is apprehended by the Divine.

Others have reported this experience of being taken up into glory also. While differing in the form and imagery, the essence of the occasion is consistently uniform. Apparently the perceptual mechanism is transposed, by-passed or over-ridden and the one having the experience is ushered into the presence of the Divine as the soul makes its way to its center and there finds its true essence with the triune God residing there, with whom it enters into an intense embrace beyond human conception. Since the normal faculties are suspended, we do not see God with our physical eyes. Our image-making function which is directly related to our earthly life is not activated so we do not behold any form. Our spiritual

---

3. First Thessalonians 4:13–18.
4. Second Corinthians 12:1–9.

eyes are blinded by the overwhelming splendor of the divine presence but our total being is flooded with a holy light accompanied by indescribable joy and heavenly happiness.

The resulting ecstasy is so intense that one is not sure whether he is "in the body or out of the body." With all the psychic faculties, emotions, and human capacities negated, the conviction that one is in the presence of God is absolute, requiring no reasoning, analysis, or consideration as to the nature of the experience. All normal operations of the mind and soul being negated and bypassed, one is consumed by the sheer immediacy of standing in the presence of God. To ask "What is happening to me?" or "Why can't I see God?" would be pathetic appeals to our human faculties to apprehend that which is beyond the human and which contains its own unique, eternal grounds for self authentication. We *know* that we are standing on the holy ground before the throne of God. This is a different kind of knowing, a "spiritual discernment" characteristic of the new epistemology of the Spirit.

When I say that I myself have been in paradise with Christ, this is what I mean. I refer to the spiritual experience granted to many in which we are so "elevated" in spirit, that we are taken up into the eternal dimension, privileged to stand in the very presence of the eternal God. Many have been invited to ". . . sit together in heavenly places in Christ Jesus"[5] or stand before the throne of the Almighty as Isaiah did when he reported that ". . . I saw also the Lord sitting on a throne, high and lifted up, and his train filled the temple."[6] Or as Paul did when he states that he was found himself in the "third heaven." John the Apostle was invited by the heavenly being to enter the transcendent dimension with the summon to ". . . Come up hither."[7] In response to this command, he entered the heavenly glory and beheld God seated on His throne in majesty surrounded by heavenly beings and received revelations of "things which must be hereafter." Isaiah and John reported that they "saw" God, but perhaps it was not with the physical eyes. In addition to Paul and John, Isaiah, Plato, Plotinus, St. Teresa of Avila, St. John of the Cross, and multitudes of others, celebrated as well as unrecognized,

---

5. Ephesians 2:6b.

6. Isaiah 6:1b.

7. Revelation 4:1–11.

have entered the transcendental dimension and beheld in some spiritual sense the divine glory.

Since this experience is wholly a matter of God's grace, being a private and personal transaction between God in Christ and ourselves, there is no technique, discipline or formulae which will guarantee its occurrence. Nor does it always require agonizing discipline with painful longing or rigid self-flagellation. It is a gift of God which may be given without the recipient meeting any specific standards or it may be withheld from those whose life has been permeated with the sincerest devotion. God's ways are higher than our ways and His thoughts higher than our thoughts;[8] therefore, our expectations and desires do not necessarily coincide with His. He never places Himself under obligation to us or allows Himself to be brought under our control.

Therefore, entering paradise with Christ is never an automatic process; the initiative is always God's. He may admit us into the presence of the heavenly glory or He may not do so, just as He pleases; our own desire and longing notwithstanding.

Nevertheless, we should conduct our devotional life so that if, at any moment either unexpected or sought with urgent longing and tears, the Door should open and we find ourselves drawn in to the heavenly glory, we would be prepared to enter, clothed in the righteousness of Christ as Paul said, "And be found in him, not having mine own righteousness, which is of the law, but that which is through the faith of Christ, the righteousness which is of God by faith:"[9]

The best preparation would seem to be absolute trust in Christ (or as near to that as we are capable) which approximates the naïve simplicity of the pristine moment when we first believed, marked by the convictional certitude that "all things are possible to him that believeth."[10] Augustus M. Toplady' phrase, "In my hand no price I bring; simply to the cross I cling"[11] from his hymn "Rock of Ages, Cleft for Me" provides a good summary of the stance that promises the most fruitful results. But in the final analysis, it all depends on God's will as to whether we receive the promise of Christ that "To day shalt thou` be with me in paradise."

---

8. Isaiah 55:9.

9. Philippians 3:9.

10. Mark 9:23b.

11. Toplady, *The Baptist Hymnal*, 342.

A vast number of people, from various walks of life, with varying understandings and interpretations of the Christian faith, have also been exalted into the realms of eternal glory and have lived to tell the story. And of course, most of the non-Christian world religions have mystical elements and many of their practitioners have sought the divine encounter and reported similar episodes in their own inner life. Apparently this opening of the door between the temporal and the eternal is a universal mystical gift to the human creature as such which God will activate when and how and to whom He will. This only causes us to proclaim His glory all the more fervently.

In the following pages, I have tried to ground this experience in the original creative act of God by which He made us *living souls* and after discussion of several spiritual exercises and practices which may help us prepare to receive the invitation, I attempt to describe my own experiences. I have undertaken this reluctantly and with trepidation because, for one thing, the inadequacy of language makes it virtually impossible to communicate such an exalted experience and secondly, the experience is so intimate and private that to tell about it seems irreverent and depreciatory.

Intermittently, over many years, my life has been marked by these divine incursions, although not with the frequency I would have wished. Like many mystics, I longed for being "caught up" into glory often but in His wisdom God does not grant us our desire. Some have noted that after a certain level of spiritual maturity has been reached and permanently established in us the ecstatic experiences which were occasional and spasmodic wholly subside.[12] After we have accepted God's calling and after He has fortified us with sufficient reassurances, He declines to allow us to become dependent on these visitations and incursions. So they gradually, at the right time after God's purpose has been accomplished, occur less frequently or not at all. We may continue to long for them but they come only in God's time and for His purpose.

What I have experienced, I can understand only as either being taken up into the heavenly place or conversely, having the divine presence permeate my localized soul.

Whether I am "up there" or He is "down here," I cannot say. Perhaps this what Paul meant by not knowing whether he was in the body or out

12. Vladimir Lossky, *The Mystical Theology of the Eastern Church*, (Crestwood, N.Y.: St. Vladimir's Seminary Press, 1976), 229–30.

of it. In either case, on either reading of it, the experience is essentially a state of being overwhelmed by the divine presence expressed as flooding Light and supernal joy. And it is always a glorious occasion for which one would totally give up ordinary life if the effects could be permanently endured. But the fragile nature of the psyche, the limited capacity of the soul makes it impossible for us to continue in this state of exaltation. In our present level of existence, we could not contain this intense glory. This is why we are assured by the scripture that "... we shall all be changed"[13] in the process of resurrection. Then, when we have been made like Him, we can enjoy His presence with us and in us forever.

Description of such experience by no means should denigrate the ordinary level of spiritual experience achieved by us as ordinary practicing Christians. We embrace the indwelling Christ in a sweet communion, receiving His grace, accepting His consolation, and thriving in fellowship with Him. His presence gives us peace and quiet power. We read about Him in our Bible and through the scripture, He speaks to us and visits us. We worship Him in church and thrill to the proclamation of His victory. The Holy Spirit warms our hearts and changes circumstances both within our hearts and occasionally in the external world. While there is glory in our daily walk with Christ, not everyone is taken up into paradise. The reason some are so chosen remains hidden in the mystery of the mind of God.

13. First Corinthians 15:51b.

2

The Divine Image and the Breath of Life

THE CAPACITY TO BE taken up into paradise, that is, to be invited to enter into the heavenly realm, is derived from the creative act of God through which we became living souls. God did not order us to come into existence with an external command or by an outwardly spoken word as He did with all the other existing things. Rather, He chose to breathe His own life into the physical form which He had shaped from the earth. The Biblical witness to His creative act affirms that ". . . the Lord God formed man of the dust of the ground, and breathed into his nostrils the breath of life; and man became a living soul."[1] The "breath of life" is in fact the breath of God; the life of man is derived from the life of God. Being endowed with the divine breath, we became living souls capable of fellowship with God and the ultimate blessing of being with Christ in paradise. Because He made us like He did, He can receive us into His presence like He does. Granting us the status of human, that is, by making us living souls, He made us capable of spiritual experience of the highest order. This spiritual experience is what I have called being with Christ *today* in paradise.

We are created then with the capacity of containing the divine presence in our own souls. It is this breath of God which is the ontological basis of our existence. This capacity is the feature of our being which enables us to be taken into the heavenly realm at the invitation of God to join Him in a face to face meeting. Being with Christ in paradise *today* is a possibility given in and with our creation as living souls. As it pleases God, anyone may be invited to join Him in His very presence in the glory of the eternal dimension. This experience takes the form of ecstatic elevation of the soul as it is being "caught up to the third heaven"[2] as the Apostle Paul calls it.

1. Genesis 2:7.
2. Second Corinthians 12:2b.

But not only is this ultimate spiritual experience grounded in the way we are created, any spiritual experience *whatever* is possible only because of our status as living souls.

Spiritual experience of any level of intensity is directly dependent on this creative act of God by which He implanted the divine image, His own life and breath, in the earthen figure He had formed of the dust of the ground. By this divine act the man Adam became a living soul. It is by this same divine act that every human person born into the world becomes a living soul. Just as He breathed the breath of life into Adam's lifeless figure, in the same manner He conveys His own life to you and me. This occurs somewhere along the way on our journey between conception and birth. At a miraculous moment in our pre-natal sojourn, when God breaths His breath into our developing form, we become a living soul, that is to say, a human person immediately endowed with all the amazing possibilities which characterize the uniqueness of human existence.

At that sacred moment, we became human. We became persons. We were instantly endowed with unimaginable capacities. Like Adam we were changed from being a mere object into a person. No longer just a physical thing, we became beings with consciousness and life, endowed with mind, personality and eternity. We became living centers of the world through which time and history would flow, being recorded and registered in our experience and the experience of God. Bearing the divine image, breathing the divine breath, we became very much like the God who gave us life. This is the way God made us; by breathing the breath of life into us, thereby implanting His image and likeness in us. If God had not made us like He did, He could not save us like He does; neither could He dwell in our hearts as He longs to do, nor could we experience transcendent life. We could not enter the divine heights to ". . . sit together in heavenly places in Christ Jesus."[3]

This creative act of God is absolutely essential, a necessary condition without which spiritual experience not occur, from the simplest warming of the heart to the most profound mystical encounter with God. And of course, we could not be the recipients of salvation for without this magnificent endowment of the image of God and His living breath, that is, without having become living souls we would neither need nor could we receive His saving grace made available through the work of Christ on

---

3. Ephesians 2:6b.

the cross and in the resurrection. This is because existing things which do not have souls neither fall into sin and therefore are not in need of being saved nor are they able to receive this saving grace. In this, we are unique in all of God's created order.

This creative event is described first in the Old Testament book of Genesis, referred to in the book of Job and explained in the New Testament in the Prologue to the Gospel of John and alluded to in other Biblical writings.

God announces His intention with this statement: "AND God said, Let us make man in our image, after our likeness:"[4] and without any hesitation He did so: "So God created man in his *own* image, in the image of God created he him . . ."[5]

In this brief account, there are no details as to the method and manner by which God replicated the image of Himself in the man lying lifeless before Him. But in the second chapter of Genesis, a story-like account is given which contains some simple but profound details, but it too is very brief. The living God creates an earthen creature, a man of dust, and then informs it with the breath of His own life. Instantly, the clay form becomes a living soul. Mind, knowledge, feeling, emotion and consciousness appeared on the earth as vital aspects and essential functions of man's life. The earth immediately became an immeasurably richer place, bringing wholly new dimensions to the creation just as God had intended. Laughter, music, and speech broke the silence of the earth. These unique characteristics of the living soul broke the silence of the earth and replaced the quietness with words, melody, logic, thought, love, and happy moments of exaltation but also the possibility of grief, depression, pathos, and weeping. The inexorable march of time and history began and the dramatic adventure of spiritual experience and transcendent life became possible. God's creation was thereby brought up to the ideal form which was in His mind when He began His momentous work. His creation now resembled Him. Now His highest creature had the capacity to share His life with God and God could now share His life with his creature. Now there were living souls inhabiting the world with whom God could have fellowship and the enjoyment that is possible only among friends who share so many things in common. God could come and visit man for now

---

4. Genesis 1:26a.

5. Genesis 1:27a.

man is like God. And God would do so! God would come and visit His creature—this man and woman whom He had made! His original visits would result in face to face conversation with man.

The breath of God becomes the spirit and life of man, that is, the basis and ground of man's vital impulse, the foundation of his existence and the essence of his personality. The breath of God in man is the dynamic power which creates and operates the unfolding inward life of man, a process which allows the creature to be human. The life of God lives in the soul of man. This life of God, that is, His breath, word, spirit or image, is the source of man's life as a living being. And this life in man is the source of all the manifold operations of the soul which includes the functions of the intellect, the spirit, the eternal part of man's existence, his capacity for self-consciousness, his ability to enter into community with fellow beings and most of all, his standing before God as responsible to God and his special status as God's friend. Because man bears the breath of God within him, worlds temporal and eternal were opened to him. He became a citizen of the cosmos, a master of the universe and a child of God. This breath gives man the special qualification to receive salvation in the fullness of time. That is, man has the potential to become a new creation in Christ. The original creation is the necessary presupposition and essential condition of the new creation. God made man like He did so that in due time He could save him like He does.

But the fact that the divine breath is the basis and ground of the soul of man does not make man divine. It makes man a human person, not a god. The breath of life is the essence of man, but it is a borrowed essence. Man's true essence does not belong to man but to God. Man's soul is derived from the life of God but there remains an "infinite qualitative difference," a difference in kind, between man and his maker. The human spirit can contain the Spirit of God without being identified with it. Man the craftsman makes an object. He does not become the object he has made. The cup contains a liquid but the liquid does not become the cup; nor the cup the liquid. The spirit of man is generated by the indwelling breath and life of God but man does not possess his source nor become identified with it. Man is made *by* God and *like* God, but the indwelling source and ground of his being is not his. It belongs to God.

The method and manner of his creation allows man to experience all the marvelous functions of Godlike personhood and most important of all, it equips him for spiritual experience, therefore enabling him to live the transcendent life. Christ can dwell in him through the act of faith and man can dwell in Christ. And he does continuing business with the Eternal who is his source. He cannot choose not to have a relationship with God, even though this may sometimes be one of negativity and defiance. Most of all, God's act of creation produced a being who can be lifted up into the inner recesses of the heavenly and receive the Light Divine, that is, the man so equipped can experience being taken up into paradise with Christ, after which he resumes a transformed life on earth for a season.

3

Our Knowledge of Eternal Space

THERE ARE UNFATHOMABLE DEPTHS within the soul; there are unimaginable heights there also. Above and below the normal stance
from which our personhood operates in ordinary life are unbound dimensions which we call "eternal space." It is beyond the capacity of the
mind to discover these deeps and it far exceeds the ability of the soul to
enter into these boundless boundaries of our being. Through intellectual
vision, Plato[1] apprehended the existence of these dimensions which he
called "the unchanging" but his vision was limited to a static state of being
which existed largely in the realm of thought. For Plato, this realm was an
idea, a concept of the mind, an implication of a metaphysical system. For
us, it is a dynamic reality, a dimension in which the creative Spirit of God
is in productive interaction with our spirit which generates our being as
human, as personality, as living souls.

But if eternal space is beyond the comprehension of the mind, beyond the conception of the imagination, how can we know of it's existence? The Apostle Paul refers to such unknowable dimensions of what
God has prepared for us. "But as it is written, Eye hath not seen, nor ear
heard, neither have entered into the heart of man, the things which God
hath prepared for them that love him."[2] Then Paul goes on to say how
we may know these things: "But God hath revealed them unto us by his
Spirit: for the Spirit searcheth all things, yea, the deep things of God."[3]

By-passing the natural eye, beyond the capacity of human hearing,
eluding the power of the *nous* (mind) to apprehend, the vision of eternal

---

1. Plato *Phaedo* 79C, trans. By Benjamin Jowett (Chicago: Encyclopedia Britannica,
Inc. 1952).

2. First Corinthians 2:9.

3. First Corinthians 2:10.

space must be revealed by the Lord if we are to know of it, and more importantly to know it experientially.

Those who have received the gift of spiritual intuition, consecrated by active faith, may be able to form a conception of the possibility of which we speak. But the surest, truest, most convincing communication of this reality comes when God Himself begins to stir in the deeps of the soul. In some mysterious dimension of our own souls, deeper than we could ever hope to reach by means of human endowments and capacities, the Lord who dwells there in an ontological capacity, may for His own purposes and in the secret councils of His own will, move within us, stirring in these ontological deeps, thus revealing His presence there in the power center of the self, where human existence as such is conveyed and activated in every being who can claim the status of human. Beyond human conception in any purely rational sense, the Spirit gives us awareness of these deeps within us.

The revelation of this reality within us with its seemingly limitless parameters and infinitely extending boundaries produces two very different responses when we are allowed to apprehend it. It both startles us with a previously unknown astonishment and at the same times seems to be the most obvious "natural" truth we have ever known. It has the "infinite qualitative difference" which separates time and eternity, which distinguishes the human and the divine, yet at the same time it is as familiar as the street we grew up on in the town we call our home.

The terms we use to describe this are quite spatial—above and below. But the experience itself seems to have this spatial quality. When God begins to stir, we become aware of the unfathomable deeps, which are both within us and infinitely removed in unheard of distances below ourselves. When we are lifted up and made to sit together in heavenly places in Christ, we become aware of heights, that are both contained within us and at the same time infinitely beyond us.

It is this "sense" of deeps and heights within us and far beyond us, which leads us to call this capacity to experience God in this way "eternal space." These dimensions are contained within us while at the same time they exceed the parameters of our existence.

When we are made aware of these deeps and this height, we are not just startled but actually and literally overwhelmed. Total submission and surrender is the only response we can make. We seem both dead and yet more alive than we could ever imagine or hope for.

We would never know that this openness to the infinite below our being and these limitless heights toward the Eternal above our being existed if we had not been granted this all encompassing and pervasive spiritual experience. As He reveals Himself, God reveals at the same time this boundlessness beneath us and these unimaginable heights above us. Thus, we find ourselves bounded by bottomless deeps below us and a spaceless canopy above us. Within those awe inspiring parameters, we live and move and have our being.

4

The Soul as a Sparkling Prism

LIGHT IS THE PHYSICAL manifestation of God. The natural eye cannot behold Him for He is enfolded in glory, "Pavillioned in Splendor"[1] and covered by the "Divine Dark."[2] The Bible presents God as light and He is encountered in mystical experience as light. Also, when He makes a rare revelation of Himself in the ontological foundations of the soul, He is perceived as light. God as He is in Himself is concealed by the brightness of His glory; the hiddenness of His full being is preserved by the splendor which surrounds Him. So we know Him as light; we receive His presence as light. This manifestation of God as light determines the characteristics of the human soul.

Just as a prism receives sunlight and breaks it into its constituent elements, producing a spectrum of color, so the soul receives the Light of God and breaks it into its constituent elements. As the prism presents a wonderful array of colors, so the soul presents a great diversity of amazing functions and capacities. Every one of our abilities is derived from the divine light, presented first in scripture as the divine breath, the breath of life and in John's Gospel as the divine presence which constitute our humanness. There it is referred to as ". . . the true Light, which lighteth every man that cometh into the world."[3]

This capacity to separate the divine light into a multitude of functions is the essential nature of the soul as living. The living soul receives divine light, breath, spirit or word and derives from that one thing a diversity of capacities which is beyond our understanding.

---

1. Robert Grant, "O Worship the King," *The Baptist Hymnal*, ed. Wesley L. Forbis, 16.

2. Dionysius the Aeropagite, *Mystical Theology*, www.esoteric.msu.edy/Vol II/Mystical Theology.html.

3. John 1:9.

The divine light empowers the intellect, activates the emotions and intuitions, and even animates the body with physical life and motion. It was not just the absence of mental and spiritual life which marked Adam before the breath of life was given. He also lacked physical life. The power to move, the physical functions of heart, lungs, feet and hands as well as all the mental and spiritual capacities are directly derived from the breath of God.

This implies that the statue-like figure of Adam had as a pre-existing capacity the prism-like potential to divide the divine gift into its multiform functions. But if so, God had included these abilities in the form He had created before He breathed into it. When God shapes earth into form, amazing transformations occur in the matter so shaped. When the form of Adam came from the hand of God, it could no longer have remained merely earth. It was earth fresh from the formative creativity of God guided by a new intention; the intention to create a being capable of being God's own friend. The breath of life would be quite capable of generating the object capable of containing it and actualizing its potential. In this case, that of dividing the light into the diverse functions of which it was capable when infused in a divinely formed human figure.

Thus man was and is a spiritual prism who receives the divine infusion of the breath of God, His own life as light, and separates it into its amazing constituent elements. This is essential feature of the human being is a living soul.

5

The Thirst for the Eternal

THE HEBREW POET WROTE "As the hart panteth after the water brooks, so panteth my soul after thee, O God. My soul thirsteth for God, for the living God: when shall I come and appear before God."[1]

The thirst for God of which the Psalm writer wrote is a universal thirst of the human heart. Augustine referred to this longing for God in his famous prayer in which he said, "Thou hast made us for thyself and our hearts are restless until they rest in thee."[2] Blaise Pascal wrote about the "infinite abyss" in the human heart which could be filled only by "an infinite and immutable object, that is to say, God Himself."[3] Pascal is often quoted as referring to a "God-shaped vacuum" within the heart. He did not actually use this terminology but the meaning is the same— that there is a longing in the soul which no earthly object can satisfy. God has reserved a place for Himself in every human heart. Therefore every human person has an undying thirst for the Eternal Presence which abides already in the heart as the *sine qua non* of humanness as such. The living soul must intentionally come into this *a priori* divine presence dwelling within it as its ground. It must enter into positive personal communion with it before peace and true joy can be found. Our souls naturally and inherently thirst for God. They long for the Living God, just as the Psalmist said.

This thirst for God is an inescapable aspect of the living soul which God breathed into the earthen figure of the first man which He had made. This act of the original creation is replicated in every human being. Somewhere along the journey from conception to birth, God breaths His own breath or life or spirit into the living thing in the womb and that

1. Psalm 42:1–2.

2. *Confessions* Bk. I, ch 1, trans. by Rex Warner (New York: New American Library, 1963).

3. *Pensees* 425, http://www.ccel.org/ccel/pascal/pensees.html, Accessed 02 June 2009.

thing then and there becomes a living soul. Until that divine inbreathing of life, the thing is just a thing. It is just a physical object until the breath of God is breathed into it. Then it becomes a human person which contains, along with other amazing characteristics and features of mind, emotions, will, desires, needs and powers, the thirst for God, and the capacity for satisfying that thirst. In committing Himself to create the human person, God committed Himself to adding His living breath; His own divine presence to the physical organism being formed in the womb of every mother-to-be. God's commitment to this self-giving act assures that every human mother's child will be human and thereby endowed with the wonderful capacities of intellect, insights, introspection, potentialities, and unimagined destinies. Every person becomes a living soul and it is God dwelling within that soul that makes this so.

The most wonderful among all the amazing operations of the soul must be this insatiable thirst for God Himself. Nothing but God can satisfy God. Nothing but God can satisfy this persistent and sometimes urgent sense of transcendental loneliness. Although it may be distorted and misunderstood by being directed toward "perishable" things such as riches, fame or fleshly satisfaction, this gnawing longing within us is for the eternal God and for Him alone. It lies deep in every human heart at the source of our being. Sin distorts our understanding of our wants and causes us to engage in useless questing for that which cannot fill the longing. It cannot be treated, cured or reduced. No therapies, medicines, counseling or psychotherapy can alleviate its effect. This is because it is a part of our being. It is an element of our essential nature. It is a part of humanness as such.

Pascal understood this unquenched thirst as a pervasive emptiness, a limitless void within, an ominous "infinite abyss." Genesis 2:7 however points to a different source of our discontent. Rather, the cause of our longing is an alienated fullness, that is to say, the creator dwells within the soul to empower it, give it life, and to sustain its identity as human, but man has become alienated from the One who gives him life and being. We ourselves have become separated from the essence of our own souls, estranged from the ontological presence of God within us. The picture is grim: man carries around in him the Eternal One, but from whom he has become alienated. The One who gave life to the soul by implanting His own life in it has become a stranger to man and considered an intruder into man's inner life. Yet God, the ground of the soul could never cease to dwell within, otherwise man would have ceased to be human and become like other elements of creation, an object, a thing. So God continues to dwell, unrecognized and unwelcome, within every living soul as the ground of its being, the source of its life. But natural man is cut off from the awareness and power of this indwelling. Even though man with his vision and understanding darkened and distorted by sin does not know who it is that is calling him to seek the unchanging reality within him, the divine presence continues and thrusts him forward to seek living fellowship with God. Man distorts this urging, confuses these impulses and seeks the passing, the transient, and the perishing. But until he comes to a faith encounter with God, his inner longing is unfulfilled and he flounders about, always seeking but never finding. The genius of man, then, is not his emptiness, not a God shaped void, not a vacuum, not an absence, not an infinite abyss but a fullness—the fullness of God which he bears around within him but which he cannot access through his own efforts and resources.

This thirst for the eternal, the permanent, the unchanging points to the living reality which constitutes the dynamic force that operates the mind, soul and personality. It is the source of aspiration, of high ideals, of heroism, of self-giving, and love. It is the basis of kinship among human beings and the connecting link with the other orders of creation. Other elements of creation were made by an external word of command. "Let there be . . ."[4] God said, and it was so. He commanded and the world stood forth. But although the human soul is created by the same word/spirit/breath/light, it was not given as an external command. Rather it was implanted inwardly; it was breathed into the heart of man and forever operates from within. In this way, God wanted to establish a special kinship and community with the human. He wanted a dwelling place on the earth and He chose the heart of man for that place of residence. And from this desire of God, man was greatly blessed to become a living soul. All the brilliance of his life derive from this intention of God.

In creating man as a person, God invites him to grandeur, heroism, vision, consciousness, truth and love and bestows on him other essential elements of personhood. Containing the spark of the divine life, the human soul provides a brilliant light in the world, a sparkling prism refracting the divine light through the manifold functions of human personality.

---

4. Genesis 1:3a.

In the Prologue to the Gospel of John the ontological presence of God is depicted under the image of light and Jesus is presented as the incarnation of the original creative breath. He is "the light that lights every man,"[5] that is, just as the breath of life conveys the quality of living soul to man in Genesis, the light that lights every man creates the soul in John's Gospel. The breath of life and the *Logos*/Light of the New Testament are the same reality. This enables us to use the metaphor of a prism to depict the function of the soul. Just as a prism refracts natural light, breaking it into its constituent parts, so the human personality divides the divine light into its manifold parts. The various functions of the human psyche are manifestations of these diverse elements of the light of God. The living soul's essential nature is seen in its capacity to receive the light and to separate it into its parts, utilizing these diverse elements to form the sparkling entity of the total self. The instant when God breathed his breath into Adam, or when he caused His own light to shine into the empty caverns of man's being, a marvelous procession of the amazing diversity of functions and capacities of the soul began to shine forth.

But personhood is also the open door to the tragic; the always present possibility of suffering, grief, disappointment, and despair. Since man carries the divine presence within himself, and reflects this radiance in his being, he must also carry within him the negative side. He also reflects the pathos of God; he also bears the possibility of pain, tragedy, and suffering.

Along with the high aspiration, the basis for longing, the vision of a transcendent dimension of life comes the possibility of being dissatisfied, unfulfilled, unhappy and sometimes quite miserable. Such unrest and dissatisfaction comes not only from falling short of the divine possibilities God implanted in us when he gave us His breath of life but also the necessity of reflecting the total image of God which includes divine pathos and God's own suffering. Requiring us to reach out, to strive, to seek and to achieve, the divine breath summons us to larger worlds, to higher realities, to dimensions of life beyond the limitations of the darkness in which we may remain. But in remaining there, we are forever discontented.

The very discomfiture we face is the evidence that the Divine lives within the soul as its source and ground. Along with the possibility of dissatisfaction, the torture of consciousness, longing and aspiring, depression

---

5. John 1:9b.

resulting from injury, rejection and repudiation along with the inescapable dimension of the tragic there are the positive fragments of love, hope, joy, and fulfillment. Some goodly degree of meaning and purpose shines through the alienation and lights up the tragic and gives us the buoyancy that bears us up. There is the music of the spheres, the glory of heroism, the beauty of the earth, the satisfactions of loving and being loved. Life is good. To be alive in God's world is to walk in grandeur. The starry heavens above and the moral law within, to use Immanuel Kant's phrase,[6] calls us forward. Brief, bright moments of wholeness and well-being, fragments of eternity shower down around us, laughter, lightness, and love lift us up. Beethoven's Fifth Symphony, Handel's Hallelujah Chorus, rational discourse, logic, mathematics and the exact sciences—all these resources cheer us, inspire us, and pull us forward.

The unsatisfied longing continues despite all of these earthly treasures. We thirst for the Eternal. We seek the Living Spring. But where shall we find it? It is within us! It has been there from the day we first began to be. It is of our own very essence, yet it is not ours! God the Eternal One who gave us life did so by giving us Himself. He dwells in every soul. He is the center! He is the source! He is the ground!

We therefore must arise and go to Him through His historical manifestation in Jesus Christ. Then we shall have the perfect peace that passes understanding which can never be found in any earthly treasure. But of course, as we have seen, He is already in us as the ground of the soul, the source of our being. Even before we are aware of this constitutive presence, He works in us and through us in various and remarkable ways. He attests to His presence, even when we do not recognize the operations of grace in us. For example, every human being has some degree of spiritual experience in addition to the normal functions of the psyche and the physical body. We all have elevated moments of eternal dimension when we are lifted up, well beyond the parameters of ordinary life. These are testaments to the fact that the breath of life, the Eternal Spirit and Word, the Divine Light is the foundation of our being and the ground of the soul. Such experience is the invitation and call to come to Him who has come to us in Jesus of Nazareth.

---

6. Kant, *The Critique of Pure Reason* (Whitefish MT: Kessinger Publishing Co., 2004), 127.

6

The Vital Center

THE CENTER OF THE soul is sacred ground which like all sacred places can only be entered in response to an invitation by God Himself. One does not intrude into one's own psychic and spiritual depths but enters only when God invites and opens the Door. Spiritual exercises, however profound they may be, do not gain access for us into the inner recesses of our own being. God is the keeper of this dimension of the soul because it is His own dwelling place. We enter only when the call of grace has been issued and the invitation has been received.

Although the soul has no physical center since it cannot be divided into parts, this truly universal gift, freely given to all is a sacred precinct, which may be thought of as a "place" in a metaphorical sense. It is not a "part" of the heart.

It is not a temporal or spatial dimension of the soul. Rather it is an ongoing relationship—a spiritual operation perpetually occurring within our own being by means of which we are being continuously created as living souls. We may draw near to this soul generating dynamic, this life giving creative action of God and "enter" for refreshment, renewal, restoration, and regeneration.

There, life is generated, our life, and from which at the same time we draw grace and salvation. To be centered means then to be in a vital and positive relationship with God who is the source and ground of our being.

Everyone who claims the status of "human" has been given this sacred place within where God dwells. This is an incomparable treasure—surpassing the most fabulous of the world's greatest riches! Everyone has it! The Lord who is gracious and good has seen to it that I possess it and you possess it and every human being possess it. For indeed, as we have said, this very presence is what makes the human being human. Therefore every being who is a living soul and active personality has it. It is the ontological basis of our existence.

Some consider that the process of merely turning inward is sufficient to enter the center of the soul. But a mere psychological motion of the self to reflect on itself is not adequate to accomplish the Biblical concept of inward communion with the Lord.

Such an arbitrary inward turning may lead the psyche to contemplate nothing more than its own mechanism and therefore mislead the one who seeks true spiritual inwardness. In this contemplation of its own processes, the soul may achieve new powers, insights and affirmations that it had not previously experienced, but this may seriously fall short of the desired meeting with God within the self.

St. Teresa of Avila points to the weakness of arbitrary inward turning without the calling and invitation of God. With incomparable precision she describes those who substitute "interior shrinking" for the true coming into the Divine presence.

> I think I have read that they are like a hedgehog or a tortoise withdrawing into itself, and whoever wrote that must have understood it well. These creatures, however, enter within themselves whenever they like; whereas with us it is not a question of our will—it happens only when God is pleased to grant us this favor.[1]

What Teresa finds so appalling is a spiritually neutral withdrawal into oneself which is under our own control and subject only to our thinking or visualizing. "Do not suppose that the understanding can attain to Him, merely by trying to think of Him as within the soul, or imagination, by picturing Him as there."[2]

When this experience of inward turning is given to us by God, however, it is an occasion for rejoicing. Teresa continues,

> Anyone who is conscious of this happening within himself should give God great praise, for he will be right to recognize what a favor it is. His response to it will open the doors for further blessings. . . . the thanksgiving which he makes for it will prepare him for greater favors."[3]

1. *The Interior Castle*, 4.3, trans. and ed. E. Allison Peers, (Garden City: Image Books Doubleday & Co., 1961).

2. Ibid.

3. Ibid.

Not confined by borders, not marked off by boundaries, this center of the soul is a constant divine-human interaction in which the Spirit of God originates, embraces, affirms, and radiates the spirit of man, making him into a living soul, that is, human. This center of the soul is the center of the universe. The breath/light of God is forever given as the ground, basis, and center of the soul. This holy transaction is a permanent ongoing function within the heart of every human being. We may think of it as a "place," a destination which we enter not by traversing physical distance but by overcoming alienation and spiritual "distance." Going there is the most marvelous journey of our lives and what we experience there is in a sense being present at our own creation.

There, life is generated, our life, and from which at the same time we draw grace and salvation. There we receive love, forgiveness, and affirmation of our own being. To be centered then means to be in a vital and positive relationship with the God who is the source and ground of our being.

Since the center of the soul is sacred ground, we must "take off our shoes" in order to approach it. That is to say, we must make the proper spiritual preparation and not attempt to come casually, otherwise the attempt will fail and we will end up contemplating ourselves. We may draw some positive results from this self-contemplation but it will fall far short of the intended meeting with God at the center, which once again, is the "place" within us where the divine Spirit/Light resides and generates our own spirits into which we can enter to receive new infusions of grace, divine power, renewed consecration, and affirmation of our being.

And since this center is a spiritual presence—the original creative presence of the living God who makes us into living souls, we enter it by means of religious exercises and spiritual commitment. That is, through devotion, contemplation, prayer, mortification of the flesh, and crucifixion of the self. Rather than a neutral psychological turning inward, repentance and faith are the instruments which conduct us to the center. After all, the center is God's presence where He generates our being. Therefore the instruments which He has appointed will bring us there.

7

Brief Bright Moments: Messages from Beyond

THE DIVINE PRESENCE MANIFESTS itself in us on many blessed occasions. We may, without any recognizable preparatory states of mind or condition, experience a strange new feeling of well-being and wonder; a sense of our oneness with the total creation. There is a quiet joy and a pervasive peace that permeates every aspect of our being and a radiant divine glow that adds a brightness to the common place and ordinary. It is as if we were at last to do that which is urged in the ancient hymn quoted by the Apostle Paul: ". . . Awake thou that sleepest, and arise from the dead and Christ shall give thee light."[1] We celebrate a sense of wellness in our own situation, at least for the precious moment of the present, and grasp a fleeting identification with all reality. We feel at one with the entire cosmos and rejoice to have a place in it. We rejoice to be alive in God's world, even though we may not know and acknowledge the God to whom it belongs.

Such experience as this does occur. It occurs because we are human beings and therefore are living souls and these feelings of exaltation are the soul's testimony to its origins and connections with the eternal reality beyond the world of time and place. This is a part of our endowment as human beings. It is an immediate shining through of the divine breath and light, which indwells every human being as such and is the ground of our existence as human. That which shines through on these occasions is the presence of God, which constitutes our being as living souls.

These occasions may be attached to some familiar object or recalled experience, a song, a poem, a Bible verse, a memory, an occasional victory in life, an overcoming of tragedy, or misfortune or other sources. But perhaps those most to be treasured are those which come to us totally

1. Ephesians 5:14.

25

"out of the blue." If we think of the eternal dimension as being "up" then this phrase gains validity. The point is that sometimes our feelings of exaltation, our sense of wholeness and well-being, have no known connection to anything we can point to. They are given wholly as an independent and free-standing gift from the Eternal, from God, and they have no known connection with any of our ordinary experiences. They occur as the result of some cause or source or completely without any known cause or source (except the graciousness of God who grants them to us). Although we may point to possible prior experiences that seem to activate these blessings, those that come unbidden, unsought, and unexpectedly, are the ones most to be prized.

If we cast our thoughts back across the time of our lives we can well remember when we were visited by such occasions and probably will be surprised at how many times we have actually had such an elevated sense of eternal realities. And if we have never had such an experience, the future is yet before us and it is full of the possibility that such experience will occur. We can hold such an expectation because we are indeed living souls, that is, human beings, having divinity as our ground with the indwelling ontological presence of God as the continuing dynamic which operates our being moment by moment. This is the promise of our nature. This is the destiny which our essence warrants to us. Let us claim the promise of our being and therefore transcend the limits of earthly existence in these selected moments chosen for us by God and granted to us by His grace.

Perhaps this cosmic feeling of which we speak was the experience of Plato, the great philosopher, which inspired him to write (speaking of the soul):

> . . . when returning into herself she reflects, then she passes into the other world, the region of purity, and eternity, and immortality, and with them she ever lives, when she is by herself and is not let or hindered; then she ceases from her erring ways, and being in communion with the unchanging.[2]

The mind "passes into another region" entering the "pure, everlasting, immortal" and is in "communion with the unchanging." Is this the movement of the soul which produces our oceanic feelings of oneness and well-being? Has our soul "returned into herself?" That may be what

2. Plato, *Phaedo* 79.

in fact occurs, perhaps below the level of our own conscious awareness. Possibly, Plato gives us a description of what in fact occurs. But be that as it may, we know that we have for the moment entered into a strange, new and wonderful dimension of reality and we celebrate the richness of this apprehension.

This new state of being, of which we are freshly aware, is vividly expressed by the more recent hymn writer who proclaimed:

> When peace, like a river, attendeth my way
> When sorrows like sea billows roll;
> Whatever my lot, Thou hast taught me to say,
> It is well, it is well with my soul.[3]

We cannot account for this strange new feeling. Nothing has changed in our everyday world as far as we know. But for no reason known to us, there is a strange and wonderful apprehension of well-being in us. It has broken upon our consciousness without warning. Without known preparation, it has made its appearance! Here it is, and it is marvelous in our eyes!

Without any conscious process of reasoning, without any subtle and persuasive arguments, we are intuitively convinced that doors long closed are about to open. Darkness, which has long ruled over our thoughts and feelings, is about to be broken up and dispelled by the light. Healing long delayed is about to step forth through some newly made conduit. Deliverance from besetting bondages seems immediately at hand.

The overcrowdedness of our inner universe has been lessened and the "stuff'd bosom" seems suddenly relieved of "that perilous stuff Which weighs about the heart."[4]

In place of overcrowdedness of the soul, there is an expansive sense of some primordial freedom. With it comes a refreshing and beautiful distance between the cares of the world and the core of our being, a glorious extrication we never thought we'd live to see! Now we feel whole—high and lifted up, elevated to the outskirts of the Eternal!

We may well congratulate ourselves. We have been visited by one of the great restoring occasions that come to us along life's way. A brief,

---

3. Horatio Spafford, *The Baptist Hymnal*, 410.

4. William Shakespeare, *The Tragedy of MacBeth* Act V, Sc.iii, ed. William Aldis Wright, (Garden City, N.Y.:Garden City Books, 1936).

bright moment from the depths of being has come to us, a messenger from the Eternal One has come to us.

This new state of apprehended well-being in which we rejoice is more than a feeling, more than a sensation. Neither reason nor emotion, it is a third faculty—a capacity of the soul to come into direct contact and communion with the Eternal without intervening steps or stages. It is by the faculty of intuition that this experience of this great moment comes to us on this most glorious day. Perhaps unable to describe that which has occurred in us, we may borrow the vivid words of Augustine, the Bishop of Hippo, in the fourth century and the greatest interpreter of the Christian faith after the Apostle Paul. Augustine wrote, after some such experience as we have referred to: "And then, in the flash of a trembling glance, my mind arrived at That Which Is."[5]

But even if we did not wake today to the sound of the music of the spheres, even if we did not greet the coming day with the smooth, quiet purring of the soul, there is no cause for despair or a bleak outlook. As a human being, we live with the constant possibility of a suddenly opened door. We all live in the immanent and ever possible unveiling of a moment "when the morning breaks eternal bright and fair."[6] This is a permanent standing possibility that is ours by virtue of our being human. This spiritual transformation of reality is a possibility given in and with the gift of humanness. So it can happen to you or me at any time and any place.

Shining moments occur to us all. Everyone has had some degree of this heightening of spiritual perspective. If we stop and think, we can surely recall many such moments of suddenly being surprised by joy. These are moments when we suddenly realize that "The morning light is breaking; the darkness disappears."[7] This can happen, not only in the morning, but also at the brightness of noon-day and in the stillness of the midnight. We have referred to it in terms of the morning only to signify the breaking of a new day of the spirit, remembering also the Biblical assurance that ". . . in the morning, then you shall see the glory of the Lord."[8]

---

5. Augustine, *Confessions* Bk VII Ch 17, trans. Rex Warner, (New York: New American Library, 1963).

6. James Black, "When the Roll is Called Up Yonder," *The Baptist Hymnal*, 516.

7. Samuel F. Smith, "The Morning Light is Breaking," *The Methodist Hymnal* (New York: The Methodist Publishing House, 1939), 487.

8. Exodus 16:7a.

Our feelings and thoughts are routine and uneventful most of the time. But this steady sameness is sometimes broken by something quite extra-ordinary. Sometimes our spirits are made to soar, perhaps just for a fleeting instant, into new heights we had not known before. Or we may have opened in us a new depth we had not previously experienced. So into the ordinary routine of the hum-drum and commonplace, exalted and elevated occasions may come. These elevated experiences occur to everyone, being an aspect of humanness itself.

These are the mountain-top moments that punctuate the ongoing ordinariness of daily life that give deepened meanings and produce changed directions. These are the special occasions in which we are overtaken by messages from another dimension. They are consolations from a realm of reality quite beyond ourselves, eternal in the heavens and resident in every human heart.

These beautifully turned bits of heavenly perfectness take many forms in their coming. They are mediated to us through many different instruments. Hitching a ride as it were on some established vehicle as in the case of a friend who said, "Something uncanny happened to me while I was listening to Beethoven's Fifth Symphony." The elevated moment came riding upon the symphonic splendor from the composer's pen and the performance of a hundred masters of their instruments.

They may come unexpectedly through other means. For instance, a human face.

When we truly grasp a human face in its strange mix of misery and grandeur, we may be grasped by a new dimension of experience, encounter a new awareness, a different apprehension of an aspect of reality. Paul Tillich pointed out this possibility to us when he wrote, "Where one is grasped by the human face as human, . . . *There* New Creation happens."[9]

This may sound very abstract but if we think for a moment we can quite possibly recall instances when the look on a human face did in fact grasp us in a strange way, arresting our thoughts, stunning us for a moment with something deep and different. Think of those rarified occasions when you were struck by some deep manifestation of humanness you had never seen before on a familiar or unfamiliar human face. That is what Tillich meant by "being grasped by a human face as human." Under certain conditions, ordinary human faces communicate a strange

9. *The New Being,* (New York: Charles Scribner's Sons, 1955), 12.

transcendent power. Quite unknown to the person being beheld, their ordinary faces become the instruments of other-worldly messages. They become vehicles for the vision of God, creating "new being" in us as we are transformed in unimagined ways.

These spiritual unveilings sometimes attach themselves in a more or less permanent and fixed way to a poem, the verse of a hymn, a Bible passage, a memory or a place. In these cases, every time we read the poem, hear the song, read the passage, recall the memory or visit the place, we receive a spiritual elevation, a sense of well-being, intimations of immortality. We can count on the blessing to come constantly and almost automatically in and through the material to which God has attached these great moments for us.

They emerge out of the ontological structure of the soul, i.e. occurring universally as derivatives of the divine breath as the ground of the soul . They come free-standing and unbidden because we are living souls. They are the birth-right of humanness, independent of religious conviction or practice. They are not only intimations of immortality but also of our humanness, coming with surprise, rejoiced in and unexpectedly without any foundations in conscious awareness.

8

A Journey Not Made with Feet or Ships

Plato wrote of a remarkable inward journey of the soul to an amazing destination.[1] He discovered that one could enter one's own soul and therein experience a transforming encounter with the Divine, communing with "the unchanging" in the realm of the "pure and everlasting, immortal and unchanging." This was more than a remarkable rational and intellectual insight. It was more than a vision; it was an apprehension of reality. It was the discovery of the essential reality of the true spiritual nature of being human and the directions for the most exalted experience of which we are capable in earthly life.

Plotinus, a later disciple of Plato, carried forward this idea of his master to exalted heights and produced the most amazing set of descriptive terms for the journey of the soul to what he called "the Fatherland." His development of this vision of Plato became the basis of Western spirituality. Plotinus said that this inward journey to an elevated inner state is not made by means of

> . . . feet, or coaches or ships for feet bring us only from land to land. Nor is it for coach or ship to bear us off. We must close our eyes and invoke a new manner of seeing, a wakefulness that is the birth-right of us all, though few put it to use.[2]

Through the work of Plotinus, Plato's philosophic vision enters into Christian theology through the philosophic movement known as Neo-Platonism. Many Christian concepts and movements have their roots in this intellectual insight of Plato and the further extension of it in the thought of Plotinus. And although many aspects of Neo-Platonism are

1. Plato, *Phaedo* 79.

2. Ennead I.6.8, *Plotinus: The Six Enneads,* trans. Stephen MacKenna and B. S. Page (Chicago: Encyclopedia Britannica, Inc. 1952).

antithetical to Christian interpretation of reality, the vision of the inward journey of the soul to "the Fatherland,"[3] which he describes as "There whence we have come, and There is The Father,"[4] apparently referring to a spiritual reality beyond time and place residing within the soul, has been influential in Christian spirituality. The quest for the inward life and mystical spirituality has been highlighted and emphasized by the Plato/Plotinus nexus.

Although the vision is impressive, the method of achieving it simply by reflection, as Plato affirms, is intellectual and therefore a process which the mind can undertake at will. By its own capacity the soul can enter into this new mode of being. For Plato the way to the "pure and everlasting, the immortal and unchanging" is thought. By the operations of the mind, one enters this eternal realm. Christian experience has discovered, however, that movements of the intellect, the rational activity of the mind, thinking and even profound thinking, does not conduct us to this central reality of the soul. Rather spiritual preparation and ultimately the inviting grace of God is the effective method of approach. Love of God, devotion to Christ, prayer, consecration, Biblical study, abandonment of the self to the Divine and, spiritually participating in the death and resurrection of Christ is the way to profound inner communion with the God who lives within the heart.

Plotinus held a similar intellectual view of the method of entry into the divine reality within the soul. A "new manner of seeing, a wakefulness that is the birth-right of us all"[5] is the required vehicle to conduct us on this inward journey. This could be interpreted in terms of the spiritual regeneration proclaimed by the Christian gospel but that is probably not what Plotinus meant since he had never embraced the Christian faith. His prescription would seem to be a matter of intellect, of thought, of rational experience rather than the reception of divine grace and therefore would fail in bringing us to the desired destination.

Nevertheless, by reflecting on the nature of the soul, Plato, Plotinus and others found that there was within them unimagined treasures of spiritual power and radiance. *Unimagined* is to be taken quite literally here for the reality they apprehended or were apprehended by is surely

---

3. Ennead I.6.8.

4. Ibid.

5. Ibid.

real and valid, not a concept, idea or effect of the imagination. The fact that this reality was apprehended by thought, by the actions of the mind, means that it was kept at a certain distance from them because the objects of thought are not matters of the heart and the experience they sought can only be apprehended by the heart. In this sense, they knew the reality they described from a distance. They were in some sense spectators of the glory they laid hold of by the action of the intellect. They could think this realm of the unchanging, this Fatherland, but ultimately it remained a thought, an intellectual concept, an idea. But the wonderful thing is that they demonstrated that through the amazing power of the intellect and the excellent capacity of the psyche, they could know of an eternal presence within the soul. Even this partial vision attests to the wonders of creation for they discovered the reality the Hebrew prophet wrote about in Genesis 2:7. They apprehended in their souls the breath of life breathed by the eternal God, the same breath that generates every human being as a living soul. They saw and spoke well of the reality they had discovered within themselves.

In a few brief sentences the Hebrew writer presents a plausible explanation of the origin of the soul which makes this inward journey possible and points to its destination—the presence of God in the soul. His account is based on revelation rather than reason and therefore has full validity for Christians. Once again we read what he writes: "And the Lord God formed man of the dust of the ground, and breathed into his nostrils the breath of life; and man became a living soul."[6]

In this account of creation, God the creator breathes the breath of life into the earthen figure he has made and the man immediately becomes a living soul. Other images are used in the Bible to depict this ontological presence of God—the word of God, the spirit of God and in the New Testament, ". . . the Light that lights every man."[7] Thus the presence of God is the ground and source of the human soul and accounts for the sacredness which we discover within us when we truly enter ourselves. And, of course, this breath of life, this life of God, is the true and only basis of the dignity that is the birthright of every human being.

The brilliant Platonic statement, based on intellectual vision and rational insight represents the highest possible development of human

---

6. Genesis 2:7.

7. John 1:9.

reason and therefore is to be admired and respected. But the Hebrew prophet's report has the force of divine revelation.

Yet the inward journey remains incomplete. The homeward trek remains unfinished. Still, the vision beckons from the distant mists and helps everyone along the way. The results of true inward turning is impressively referred to by an American spiritual writer who said: "When the soul enters into her Ground, into the innermost center of her being, divine power suddenly pours into her."[8]

But only since the historical coming of Jesus Christ has it become possible to enter fully into the sacred ground of the soul. Only through Him can we enter into the inner precincts of our being and taste the heavenly glory in this present life. But it must not be supposed that Jesus Christ is only the instrument who leads us to the center. He is not the way to the center. He is, in fact, the center itself. Having become the locale of the entire Godhead bodily, He is the destination we seek. He is the object of our quest. It is to Him that we go to find the center of reality, the center of our own being, the center of the universe. As Paul the Apostle profoundly described Him:

> Who is the image of the invisible God, the firstborn of every creature: For by him were all things created, that are in heaven, and that are in earth, visible and invisible, whether they be thrones, or dominions, or principalities, or powers: all things were created by him, and for him: And he is before all things, and by him all things consist. And he is head of the body, the church: who is the beginning, the first born from the dead; that in all things he might have the preeminence. For it pleased the Father that in him should all fullness dwell;[9]

Not just the way to the center then, the risen Christ, the Eternal Son and savior, is the very center itself. The act by means of which our salvation is completed and confirmed is the personal indwelling of Christ within our hearts. This coming possibility was in His heart, on His mind and often on His lips. And when He comes into our hearts, the fullness of the entire Godhead, the blessed Trinity of Father, Son and Holy Spirit enters to dwell. His entrance into our heart performs the union of the ontological and the redemptive in us and activates the divine reunion which

8. Rufus M. Jones, *Some Exponents of Mystical Religion,* (New York: The Abingdon Press, 1930), 102.

9. Colossians 1:15–19.

produces an ecstasy beyond compare in our hearts. The ontological presence which has been the basis of our being as long as we have existed is joined with the historical work of redemption performed by Jesus Christ in the cross and resurrection. This entrance is the consummation of the salvation He has acquired for us when we receive Him by means of grace through our faith.

When the believer himself is incorporated in the divine reunion occurring within his own heart, the power that floods his soul from that moment and through that unity is shed abroad through his entire being resulting in ecstatic recognition of activated Godhood as the soul is overwhelmed by floods of grace divine.

Turning our eyes upon Jesus therefore is a turning of our inner eyes upon Him. Looking into his face involves an interior seeing. Praising Him is a shout turned inward for His ears with which He will hear us are in our own hearts. Walking with Him is an inner walk, for His feet tread no longer the dusty roads of Galilee, but the streets of the heavenly city and the avenues of our own souls. The flood-gates of grace and love are opened within us and from them emerge all the blessings of God to us. And we bear about within us, not only His triumphant victory, the power of His resurrection, but also the fellowship of His suffering resulting from His excruciating crucifixion.

No wonder that we want to make this inward journey. We seek the source from which all blessings flow, the font of all mercy and lovingkindness, the living stream of all that matters and the totality of the really real.

9

There You Will See Him

HOW CONVENIENT THE GRACIOUS Lord has made it for you and me! How easy He has made it for us to come into His presence. Why, we do not even have to leave "home" to find Him! That is, we do not have to leave the boundaries of our own souls to come face to face with Christ the savior. What a terrific blessing this is! Think of it! We can come to the eternal God within our own selves without having to venture out into the vast universe; without having to make a journey through the immensity of time and space! He has been within easy access and reach from the very moment we first believed. And we locate Him and approach the inward throne of grace while remaining in the familiar security of our own hearts! He has promised never to leave us nor forsake us. He has promised never to leave us alone. He has said, ". . . I am with you alway; even to the end of the world . . ."[1] And He is absolutely faithful; He has kept the promise with a holy and eternal commitment.

That is where we find Him—in our own hearts! That is where we commune with Him! That is where we rejoice in Him! That is where we receive the abundance of His grace! That is where we receive His overflowing and restoring love! That is where we know Him in the fellowship of His suffering and in the power of His resurrection! Where? In our own hearts. That is where He lives! That is His dwelling-place. In your heart and mine, sometimes broken and contrite! Sometimes overflowing with jubilation and praise. Sometimes with moving solemnity and the awesome sense of holiness and at other times with the intimacy of the dearest friendship. But He is always there within us with an unwavering constancy—Jesus Christ is always with us!

So we must never look for Him anywhere else.

1. Matthew 28:20b.

When some say, "He is in the desert! We saw Him there!" do not believe it.

When they say, "We saw Him on the mountain. There you will find Him!" Do not believe this report. Do not climb the mountain. Do not seek Him in the heights!

When they say, "We have seen Him walking on the water!" Do not be mislead; do not be beguiled.

When they exclaim, "Let us go up into the heavens to bring Him down!" pay no attention to such pretense.

"Lo, here! Lo, there!" they may proclaim. But no! Do not seek Him in diverse places, exotic locations with strange sounding names.

Rather seek Him where He can be found. Seek Him in His true house and home! Look for Him at His true and certain dwelling-place—in your own heart. Turn inward to your own sacred space which He himself has created. Find Him in the temple He has established in your own heart! Go to the place He has appointed as the site of a continuing rendezvous. He wants to meet you there! Within your own heart you will find Him whom thou seekest. For He has promised to be there always!—that is, in your own heart! There you will be embraced by a holy warmth and powerful light that you never imagined to exist. There you will receive grace and empowerment beyond anything you have ever imagined, beyond the any possible conception of your heart and mind. There you will receive assurances and affirmation beyond your fondest dreams. There you will be received into a fellowship and friendship that surpasses any thing on earth or heaven!

When we enter into the sacred precinct of the soul where Christ dwells, marvelous transformations occur—the commonplace becomes holy; the ordinary becomes sacred. The clothes we are presently wearing become sacred garments, the sacerdotal robes which adorn us as we come into His presence. Every common shrub becomes a burning bush aflame with God. Every rose reflects the His crimson sacrifice for sin on Calvary. Every lily glistens with the whiteness of His purity. When we come to Him in the place He has appointed, He provides for our eyes heavenly spectacles which allow us to see everything from His point of view. We now behold everything under the aspect of eternity; from an eternal perspective so that we see Him everywhere and everything communicates His power and testifies to His glory. And most importantly we view every person as one for whom Christ died and in whom He longs to dwell. Such ecstatic moments with Christ lead us to the mountain top from which we view the world, life and the totality of reality from God's point of view and on leaving the mountain, we find ordinary moments are now filled with resurrection glory!

Now we see that when we come into our own hearts or enter into the deeps of our own self with the consecrated intention, He will most assuredly meet us there, just as He promised His disciples immediately after His resurrection. "Then saith Jesus unto them, be not afraid: go tell my brethren that they go into Galilee, and there they shall see me."[2] The angel had previously announced ". . . he goeth before you into Galilee; there you shall see him . . ."[3] In the same way, He has gone before us into our own hearts and *there* He will meet us.

2. Matthew 28:10.
3. Matthew 28:7b.

10

Come Totally Alone and Jesus Will Meet You There

WE MUST NEVER TAKE anything to heart—except ourselves! What is the meaning of "heart" in this context? By "heart" we mean the deeps of the self/soul where life's greatest blessing and empowerment occurs. It is the very residence of God, the "place" where He dwells on earth. These are the sacred dimensions of our being; the sacred room where only God and ourselves can dwell.

Taking *only* ourselves to heart, we will come face to face with God without variation or shadow made by His turning. However, if we take anything else into the sacred room we may create one of two results— first, the fellowship God intended to have with us within our own hearts is reduced, hindered or totally obliterated. And second, there is formed a spiritual vacuum or void within the heart into which all manner of spiritual and emotional distress and disturbance may come.

Therefore, nothing but ourselves alone must be allowed to enter the sacred room, that is, be taken to heart. Worry, stress, disappointment, anger, hatred, desire for vengeance, lust, self-interest, and the like must be dealt with outside the heart. Positive concerns such as care for fellow human beings, hunger and thirst for righteousness, sympathy for the sick and bereaved, empathy for those treated unjustly, compassion for helpless children caught up in poverty and violence, patriotism and love for our national heritage, our own goodness and spiritual well-being, these and all other interests and concerns, even our ultimate concerns, are to be kept external, outside the sacred room, dealt with outside the heart.

Nothing is to be taken with us when we enter the inner recesses of the heart. Nothing is to enter these sacred precincts of the soul but ourselves alone. No expectations, no demands, no requests for solutions, no desire for anything. We enter our heart for one thing only—to rejoice with God and in God. One must therefore achieve a radical singularity, an absolute aloneness, like that required of Moses before he could approach God on Mount Sinai. "And Moses alone shall come near the Lord; but they shall not come nigh; neither shall the people go up with him."[1]

When we leave the sacred place, the cares we resume will be much lighter for they will have been put in spiritual perspective and you will be given a renewal of spiritual power. This is possible because of the *spiritual I*, the unadorned self, detached from all its predicates and interests, reduced to its bare essence, alone is to enter into the sacred place within, that is, "the heart."

The purpose of this divine indwelling is very restricted, very exclusive. Although the Psalm writer had a different understanding of the process, he understood and longed for the results which only God could produce when he prayed:

> Create in me a clean heart, O God; and renew a right spirit within me. Cast me not away from thy presence; and take not thy holy spirit from me. Restore unto me the joy of thy salvation; and uphold me with thy free spirit.[2]

The Psalmist sought the restoration of spiritual powers, the reaffirmation of the soul, the renewal of the mind, the strengthening of faith, the empowering of righteous resolve, the restoration of friendship with the Eternal, the enhancement of joy and the activation of praise. The showering of our lives with grace, the equipping of ourselves for spiritual service, the submerging of the self in Godlikeness—these are the things we receive there in our meeting with God in our own hearts. These benefits are not to be deliberately sought. Remember, all desire is to be left outside the sacred room. If we enter into His presence within with an agenda, a program, a list of blessings desired, then the entire transaction is reduced to a self-seeking operation and nothing will result. Our disinterest must be total; all desire must be purged, even the desire for spiritual blessing and divine embracement.

Bringing cares, burdens and problems into the sacred room will only hinder and eventually destroy this fellowship God intended. If we come without this blessed singularity, this godly *aloneness*, the flow of grace is hindered and we do not receive the blessing.

---

1. Exodus 24:2.
2. Psalm 51:10–12.

With this radical singularity, we enter the very residence of God, the "place" where He dwells on earth given in and with the creation of the first man into which He blew His breath/life by means of which man became human.

The deep self has a marvelous faculty for the enrichment of life and the extension of the powers of the self beyond anything we could think or imagine. It is a resident power for the miraculous within us. We address it in a paean of praise:

> O Deep Self! O Miraculous Mind! What a glorious assignment God has given to you in the order of creation! How truly did the Psalmist confess when he apprehended you: "I am fearfully and wonderfully made!"[3] You are a ready source of life's greatest riches; a reservoir of heaven's grandest treasures; a broadening channel of grace when rightly entered. You are a standing source of the unimaginable and the seemingly impossible! You are the Temple of God on earth! When I come to you as truly *I*, I am in the third heaven; I sit together with Christ in heavenly places. And you are closer to me than my own *I*. You are the dwelling place of God in me, you are the residence of Christ in me, you are the Temple of the Holy Spirit in me! For there, Myself and God together are forever intertwined.

3. Psalm 139:14b.

11

To Those Who Suppose He Has Left Them

W E MAY SAY, " I have gone within but I did not find Him." To this we must reply in the words of Meister Eckhart: "God is within; we are without. God is at home; we are abroad."[1] Meister Eckhart is correct. If there is any absence within us, it is our absence. If no inward communion occurs, it is we ourselves who are absent, not having entered into the place of treasure at the center of the soul.

We may continue our complaint: "I once had Him but I lost Him. I once knew Jesus as a friend, but I became a stranger. I once rejoiced in His presence, but now I feel only an emptiness and a void within myself where once His glory dwelt."

We must be reminded that the treasure He has given us is never taken away. Jesus is still within us! The Holy Spirit is still dwelling in God's temple in our heart. The Father is still a resident of the sacred space of our heart. So if we have lost Him, it is truly we ourselves who have created the crisis. He has not left us; we have left Him! But the loss is not complete and final. This loss of awareness is tentative and temporary. And that is just what it is—a loss of awareness, not a loss of the essence of the soul; such a loss is only the loss of a subjective comfort; not the loss of the essential reality of our existence. On what grounds can this be said? Just this: ". . . for he hath said I will never leave thee, nor forsake thee nor thee."[2] This promise is absolutely secure and cannot be revoked. It is as certain as any commitment made by the eternal God who cannot go back on any assurance He has given us. So Jesus Christ is always both *with* us and *within us*.

---

1. Raymond B. Blakney, *Meister Eckhart: A Modern Translation,* (New York: Harper & Row,1941), 132.
2. Hebrews 13:5.

The great spiritual writers of the Middle Ages have dealt with this problem and have formulated what appears to be a true and valid answer to this feeling of having lost Him. They say we have lost Him *within ourselves*. We have "lost" Him within our own house and home! He still resides in the heart, not outside. Just like the widow who lost her precious coins of whom Jesus spoke. She had lost them in her own house. She did not have to sweep the barn, search the countryside, scale the mountain or descend into the sea to find them. She found them where she had lost them—in her own house.

The ancient mystic of England, Walter Hilton, reminds us that Jesus shows His grace to us even in placing limitations on where He will allow us to lose Him! He will allow Himself to be lost only within our own selves. He allows Himself to be misplaced only within the confines of our own hearts where the possibility of being found again is always imminent. What mercy! What love! Walter Hilton said:

> This was His mercy, that He would suffer Himself to be lost only where He can be found. You do not need to run off to Rome or to Jerusalem to look for Him there: turn your thoughts into your own soul, where He is hidden."[3]

We must remember now that the treasure He has given us is not ever taken away. Jesus is still within us! The Holy Spirit is still dwelling in God's temple in our heart. The Father is still a resident of the sacred space within our heart. So if we have lost Him, it is *we* who have lost *Him*. He has not left us; we have left Him! Leaving Him consists primarily in this: we no longer allow Him to be the lord of our lives, the king of our hearts. He continues to dwell within us but we do not give Him dominion over our hearts and lives. When we think that He has left us what has happened is that now we rule our own lives. He is still within our hearts but we have relegated Him to a subordinate status. He stills lives within us but we do not allow Him to rule over us. When I assert that "I am the Captain of my fate; the master of my soul,"[4] I have assumed lordship over my life and have displaced Him from His central position in my being. If He had truly

---

3. Walter Hilton, *The Scale of Perfection* Bk. I ch. 49, ed. Eric Colledge (New York: Charles Scribner's Sons, 1961).

4. William Ernest Henley, "Invictus," *British Literature from Blake to the Present Day*, vol 2, eds. Hazelton Spencer, Walter E. Houghton and Herbert Barrows (Boston: D. C. Heath and Company 1952), 869–70.

left us in His capacity as savior and redeemer, we would be of all persons most miserable, lost and undone. But if He had left us as the ontological ground of the soul, our humanness would have exited with Him since the indwelling divine presence is the essential presupposition of our existence as human. When He is supposed to have left us *ontologically,* our status as human would have left at the same time and we would now be nothing more than any other object of nature.

Just as Jesus Christ is the same yesterday, today and forever,[5] He never leaves us once having entered as savior. And of course, if He would leave the ontological ground of the soul, we would cease to be human and become a beast of the field. He dwells there even now in the presence of the eternal Father and the blessed Holy Spirit with unvarying certainty and unwavering constancy.

Even though we may not be on friendly terms with Him, He is nevertheless still in our hearts both as the ground of our being and, in addition, as savior if we once accepted Him as such. We may be morally and ethically absent from His presence within us. We may be, and quite often are, like Adam and Eve in the Garden of Eden eager to separate ourselves from Him because of our sin and guilt. There may be many barriers between ourselves and God in this sense. So we may not be at home to ourselves because we prefer to be absent. We choose to be not at home to ourselves. But absences of this sort, resulting from such causes, are never final and ultimate. We may be alienated from Him, but He is still there.

5. Hebrews 13:8.

12

Divine Embracement

"I WILL ARISE AND go to Jesus, He will embrace me in His arms; In the arms of my dear Savior, O there are ten thousand charms."[1] The hymn asserts that Jesus will embrace us when we arise and go to Him.

While we "go" to Him on the first occasion of our faith as we reach out to Him as we hear the historical gospel, thereafter we "come" to Him for from that pristine moment when we first believed, He dwells within our hearts. So we "come" to Him by turning inwardly to commune with Him. By coming to our own selves, by entering our own souls, we find Him waiting to embrace us as we embrace Him.

To embrace a beloved is the most intimate act that can occur between two persons. This occurs at the human level between parent and child, husband and wife, lover and the beloved. And since we can speak of the Divine only in human language and ordinary terms, we can speak of our most intimate relationship with God as embracing Him and being embraced in return.

We are using the term "embrace" here to indicate the most mystical and exalted encounter between ourselves and God that can occur. When we "arise" and come to Jesus who dwells within us, "He will embrace us in His arms." As we embrace Him, He embraces us.

But of course, Jesus has been embracing us from the moment we first became living souls. Indeed, His embrace of us while we were yet in our mother's womb is what gave us life and being in the beginning of our existence as persons. The divine act is always prior to the human act. As the Apostle John says, "We love him, because he first loved us,"[2] so we embrace Him because He first embraced us, and we come to Him

---

1. Joseph Hart "Come Ye Sinners, Poor and Needy," *The Baptist Hymnal* 323.
2. First John 4:19.

because He first came to us. He has been with us and in us as long as we have been in existence and in fact His presence is the source and ground of our existence. When God breathed His own breath into the earthen figure of Adam, the man became a living soul. That act was the prototype of our own situation. When God breathed into the undeveloped form which was ourselves, we became living souls. By that act we were granted the privilege of living in the everlasting divine embrace. We can therefore act to embrace Him, awakening from our slumber, stirring up the gift that is within us, arising and coming to Jesus. Since He has always had us in His embrace, we need only to reach out to Him to complete the loving transaction. His arms already enfold us, so now we must enfold Him in our spiritual arms.

Even so, the scripture refers specifically to the suffering of God. The Bible says that pathos, regret and grief entered His heart when He saw how the man He had so lovingly made by sharing His own life with the earthen figure had fallen into sin. The Hebrew poet wrote:

> And God saw that the wickedness of man was great in the earth, and that every imagination of the thoughts of his heart was only evil continually. And it repented the Lord that he had made man on the earth, and it grieved him at his heart.[3]

There was grief in heaven; sorrow in the life of the Eternal; pathos in the heart of the Divine. This is a tragic consequence of sin. This conduct of mankind pierced the very heart of God and disrupted the plans and intentions of heaven. Who could have imagined that apparently simple disobedience to God could have resulted in such cosmic disruption? There must be more to sin than we ever imagined. We must consider ourselves as among those who are included in Anselm's remark to Boso when he said, "You have not as yet estimated the great burden of sin."[4] Later we refer to short prayers that "pierceth heaven" but perhaps we have never thought of sin as piercing heaven and effecting the very heart of God. But He was "grieved . . . at his heart."

So God desires to be embraced by us. According to the Bible, God needs to be enfolded in our love for Him just as we need to be enfolded in

---

3. Genesis 6:5–6.

4. Anselm Cur Deus Homo Bk First, Ch XXI, *Basic Writings: Proslogium; Monologium; Guanilo's on behalf of the fool; Cur deus homo,* trans. Sidney N. Deane, 2nd ed. (La Salle Il: Open Court Publishing Co., 1961).

His love for us. We embrace God and bring joy in heaven by repentance and faith in Jesus Christ as savior and lord. For indeed Jesus Himself said; "Likewise, I say unto you, there is joy in the presence of the angels of God over one sinner that repenteth."[5] Joy in heaven replaces the grief of God.

When we embrace Christ, we embrace God as Father, Son and Holy Spirit. The trinity of persons in the Godhead is an eternal distinction and not produced by diversity of function, division of labor, or historical considerations. When God generates Himself in an eternal process of generation, He does so as three persons. There is oneness of essence in the Godhead. There could therefore never be conflict or division between the three persons. For all of its seriousness, sin did not cause any disruption between Father, Son and Holy Spirit. When God breathed the breath of life into man, it was God: Father, Son and Holy Spirit. After Jesus became incarnate, Paul says, "For in him dwelleth all the fullness of the Godhead bodily."[6] So it was God as Father, Son, and Holy Spirit who appeared as Jesus of Nazareth. They are one in substance, essence, purpose, goal, and the intention to save the human family and bring it in to fellowship, friendship and harmony with itself.

This mystery of the triune God is hidden in what some have called Divine Dark.[7] We know nothing of God as He is in Himself. We know only what He has revealed about Himself. He has revealed He is one God in three persons but He did not tell us how this could be. It is a mystery to the intellect and a bafflement to human understanding. It is an aspect of God's unrevealed life; the hidden inner relationship of the elements of His being. It is accepted by faith while not being fully understood by the mind. God saw no need or desirability of disclosing more information than is contained in scripture. So there is no word from the Lord on this.

Dionysus the Aeropagite offers the intriguing notion that the hiddenness in God is the result of His splendor overwhelming the faculties of the beholder with blinding light.[8] The hymn writer reflects this idea when he described God as "Pavillioned in splendor, and girded with praise."[9] Moses was instructed not to look upon God. The brilliance of His Glory is

5. Luke 15:10.

6. Colossians 2:9.

7. Dionysius the Aeropagite, ch. 1.

8. Ibid.

9. Robert Grant, "O Worship the King," *The Baptist Hymnal*, 16.

blinding. He is hidden by His own splendor, majesty, and radiance. Thus, the divine dignity is maintained not by exclusiveness or aloofness but by His own attributes of holiness, brilliance and glory.

There was no *nothingness* before God. There is no beginning or end; no temporal parameters in "eternal." So there was never a time when God was not, just as there was never a time when the Father was not, or when the Son was not, or when the Holy Spirit was not. The nonexistence of God is unimaginable, the pre-existing dark is impossible, and the beginning of God is inconceivable. The cunning of reason always brings us back to the beginning of the circle where we began.

There was no conflict either within the Godhead or between God and some primordial darkness. But there was a conflict in the relationship of God to man. This, of course, was caused by man's disobedience. It is directly attributable to sin. This disruption in God's plans has already been discussed and indeed, is the entire presupposition of this book

However, a reunion occurs in the experience of God Himself when we embrace Christ His son as Savior. It is not an event within the being of God; not a transaction within the Godhead. God is always *one*, but one in three persons, having the same substance, essence and attributes.

The division to be overcome is between the ontological function and the redemptive function. If God is in us as the ontological ground of the soul as the scripture says and Christ dwells in our hearts by faith, then some sense of Divine Reunion is inescapable. Because of man's sin, God's redemptive work is externalized. He can no longer save from within. The human soul has been beset with blockages and obstructions to the flow of inward grace. God must come to man externally; through the historical stream, subject now to man's actions of believing, trusting, and accepting. As the ontological presence is *a priori*, not depending on human concurrence, irrevocable, and indestructible, so the redemptive presence is subject to the subjective whims of man and totally dependent on man's willing acceptance. So God comes through theophany, confrontations on the plains of Mamre, wrestling in the night with wayward fugatives, writing law on tablets of stone, sending messages through prophets and visions to seers, elaborate temple rituals and services, slaughterings and sacrifices, and finally through the incarnation of His own son. All the while He is dwelling in the depths of the human soul as the pristine and pure divinity who is generating the human soul as such. But in history, He has subjected Himself to the preferences of sinful man.

This situation of the dual presences of God in human life is the result of sin which made this reunion necessary. It is these two relationships of God with man that must be reconciled. They are the elements of the Divine Reunion. The ontological indwelling of the breath of God which creates the human soul as human and gives it status as a living soul capable of fellowship and friendship with God must be reconciled with the second of these relationships. That is, the indwelling of Christ in the heart based on faith in the external work of Christ in redemption. The first of these divine presences makes man human; the second makes man Christian. The Divine Reunion is the joining together these two, first in the heavenly realm as Christ finished His redemptive work and the second is the joining together of the redemptive and ontological in the human person. The very possibility of this joining of the creative and redemptive presupposes that the person, through hearing the gospel, repentance, and the exercise of personal faith chooses Christ as savior who then becomes a resident of the heart. Then and there, the ontological and the historical, creation and redemption are united into a harmonized entity. The Divine Reunion. which occurred when Jesus Christ took His seat at the right hand of the Father, is recapitulated within the individual believer and the kind of joy that reigned in heaven is reproduced in the believer's soul. The joy in heaven spills over on earth in the believer's heart.

Between the grief in God's heart and the rejoicing in heaven there is a monumental amount of work and sacrifice. It reached its apex in the incarnation of Christ which culminated in the cross and resurrection. The Hebrews letter tells us that ". . . this man, after he had offered one sacrifice for sin for ever, sat down at the right hand of God;"[10] Through belief in the proclamation of the gospel the joy in heaven becomes joy on earth. And Jesus prays as recorded in the gospel,

> Neither pray I for those alone, but for them also which shall believe on me through their word: That they all may be one; as thou, Father, art in me, and I in thee, that they may also be one in us: that the world may believe that thou hast sent me. . . . I in them, and thou in me, that they may be made perfect in one . . ."[11]

So when we arise and go to Jesus, embrace Him and are embraced by Him, heaven and earth respond. The joy of heaven overcomes a degree

---

10. Hebrews 10:12.
11. John 17:20–21, 23.

of the divine pathos; any grief that remains in God's heart is for those who have not embraced His son's saving work. The joy of the Reunion in heaven is recapitulated in our hearts, and overflows into the world. The believer becomes a participant in the Reunion as Jesus prayed. On earth our hearts sing with the songs of the Zion above.

13

Practicing the Presence

COMING TO GOD IS a single function of the soul and a seamless garment without division, but it can be thought of as a two-fold process.
Two distinguishable steps are presented in the Bible which may bring us
into His presence and therefore complete the embrace. The first step is
an inward turning toward our own hearts—a coming home to our own
souls where we find the indwelling presence of the Spirit of God waiting
to embrace us in a gracious friendship. The second is an upward casting
of all our care on Him, an external act of referring every grief, burden,
sickness or distress on the Lord as He dwells around us and above us. For
God is both within us and above and around us. Both of these steps have
been referred to previously in this writing but we now recapitulate and
join them into a single function.

Inward turning and upward casting of care, then, are the avenues by
which spiritual experience of every level of intensity comes to us. Both
avenues are involved whether we are aware of them or not, whether we
activate them intentionally or not, in every upward movement of the soul
toward God. All Christian experience which all believers share, from the
basic dynamics of conversion to saving faith to the exalted experience of
being taken into the 'third heaven" as Paul was, consist of inward turning
to Christ and casting of our care on Him. While we may not at the time be
able to distinguish these as elements as distinct steps of the transformation
which is occurring in us, they are contained in the act of accepting Christ
through repentance and faith as well as the higher reaches of the soul as it
enters into personal and intense interaction with God in Christ.

The whole gamut of encounter with the Divine, from the gentle
warming of the heart, such as John Wesley reported as occurring to him

at the Aldersgate meeting,[1] to the overwhelming flooding of the soul as multitudes of Christians have been privileged to receive results from these two operations, which as we have said are actually one thing. Once again, these are inward turning to the indwelling presence of God in Christ and parallel to this, the casting of all our care on Him, because as the Apostle Peter says, ". . . he careth for you."[2]

Intense elevated "mystical" encounters with the Divine are often sought through specific and deliberate practice of these two operations. When one feels drawn to the divine presence in a special way, then the dynamics of coming to God will be discovered to consist of inward turning and upward casting of care. But sometimes the highest experience is that given wholly unsought as when we are surprised by God's gracious outpouring of His Spirit upon us, even though we had not consciously prepared ourselves for it and perhaps had not even known that such overwhelming experience of God was possible. It will be discovered on reflection on this kind of blessing that we had been practicing the art of inward communion with the indwelling Christ and also referring all our troubles, cares and concerns to Him. We had been doing this as an ongoing expression of our faith on the basis of which God surprised us by flooding our lives in special occasions of overwhelming joy, power, and grace. We were, like the Apostle Paul, taken up into the heavens to behold Him in visions of glory.

We will divide the subject at this point. The remainder of this chapter will consider turning inward; while the next one will treat the upward casting of our care, or referring everything to God.

John of Ruysbroeck treats the question of inwardness. Comparing Christ to the sun who provides divine brightness and by His Spirit engenders a ". . . fiery ardour by His incoming, enkindles every ready, free and uplifted heart."[3] This *fiery ardour* produces a unity of the heart which cannot be produced unless "the Spirit of God blows to a flame His fire in our hearts. For this fire makes one with itself and like to itself all that it can

---

1. John Wesley, "Extracts from John Wesley's Journal, 8th January to 24th May 1738," *John and Charles Wesley*, ed. by Frank Whalen (New York: Paulist Press, 1981), 107.

2. First Peter 5:7b.

3. John of Ruysbroeck *Adornment of the Spiritual Marriage* Bk.II ch VIII, trans. by C.A. Wynschenk Dom, ed. Edith Underhill (CCEL\r\ruysbroe\adornmen\adornmen \htm 2000).

master and re-shape."[4] This spiritual fire thus produces unity of heart by mastering and reshaping everything in the heart to resemble itself. Then ". . . a man feels himself to be gathered together with all his powers in the unity of his heart."[5] Inward peace and restfulness of heart result; body and soul are drawn together; heart and senses are unified, outward and inward powers are "enclosed . . . in the unity of love."[6]

And finally, the great transaction results in wonderful inwardness:

> From this unity springs inwardness; for none can be inward save him who is gathered together in unity within himself. Inwardness means that a man is turned within, into his own heart, that thereby he may understand and feel the interior workings, and the interior words of God. Inwardness is a sensible fire of love, which the Spirit of God has blown to a flame, and which urges a man from within; and he knows not whence it comes nor what has befallen him."[7]

In summary, Ruysbroeck thinks of the Spirit as kindling a fiery presence in the heart which appears as an intense *ardor*. This presupposes a heart that is prepared and ready for this occurrence. The Spirit blows upon the prepared coals and causes them to flare up into a raging fire. This fire melts and reshapes the content of the heart; making it like itself. This reshaping of the heart and its contents produces unity by gathering together all the elements contained there. Unity produces peace as body and soul, inner and outer powers are harmonized and "enclosed in the unity of love." This unity produces inwardness by turning the person within, toward his own heart. Then he understands and feels the interior workings and words of God. Then, as Ruysbroeck says above: "Inwardness is a sensible fire of love, which the Spirit of God has blown to a flame, and which urges a man from within . . ."

Although he utilizes a lot of symbolism in his presentation, in the short form Ruysbroeck is saying that inwardness is a spiritual situation which the Holy Spirit brings about by activating and energizing man's desire to know God inwardly. *Ardor* or spiritual enthusiasm, fanned into flame by the Spirit melts the heart and produces unity or oneness which is the essence of inwardness.

4. Ibid., Bk II ch IX.
5. Ibid.
6. Ibid.
7. Ibid., Bk II ch X.

The elaborate complexity of Ruysbroeck's insight will be contrasted considerably with the simplicity of the two Quaker positions presented below.

In his devotional classic, Thomas Kelley gives some very useful strategies which may lead to the inwardness we desire. He asks the question of how we are to practice the life of prayer without ceasing. His answer is precise and specific: "By quiet, persistent practice in turning of all our being, day and night, in prayer and inward worship and surrender, toward Him who calls in the deeps of our souls."[8] This must be repeated until an "inward orientation" as a habit of mind is established. It will not be a steady ascent, but steadiness can be attained through weeks, months and years of attempts, failures and attempts again.

No prior preparation is necessary, according to Kelley. Therefore, one can begin at once. The practice can be begun immediately and the journey toward inwardness starts when we wish and right where we are. Inward turning in Kelley's view is open to instant practice. "Begin now, as you read these words, as you sit in your chair, to offer your whole selves, utterly and in joyful abandon, in quiet, glad surrender to Him who is within."[9]

When one lapses or forgets, which will be a frequent and painful occurrence in the beginning, one must not fall into despair. Of course, there will be differences of accomplishment in the process of inward worship. Some quickly achieve ". . . an amazing stayedness in Him, a well-nigh unbroken life of humble quiet adoration in His presence . . . Here is not ecstasy but serenity, unshakeableness, firmness of life-orientation."[10]

This inward turning, understood in this way, requires no asceticism or striving for mystical advancement. It is open to anyone because everyone is inhabited by the divine light. Kelley insists there is no technique for achieving this state of being "at Home in Him."[11] The goal is to move toward greater and greater simplicity in spoken prayer and finally to achieve an attitude of prayer and worship which makes verbalization unnecessary. As one advances toward that goal, simple, whispered words

---

8. *The Testament of Devotion*, (New York: Harper & Row, 1941), 38.

9. Ibid., 38.

10. Ibid., 42.

11. Ibid., 43.

such as *Thine only, thine only* may occur spontaneously, or one may lay hold of a fragment of scripture and repeat it inwardly over and over.[12]

A similar approach to inwardness is advanced by the little Quaker devotional book, compiled anonymously, entitled *A Guide to True Peace.* The authors state that:

> You should consider yourself as being placed in the Divine Presence, looking with a single eye to him, resigning yourself entirely into his hands, to receive from him whatsoever he may be pleased to dispense to you, calmly endeavoring, at this time to fix your mind in peace and silence, quitting your own reasoning, and not willingly thinking on anything, how good and how profitable soever it may appear to be. And should any vain thoughts present themselves, you should gently turn from them; thus faithfully and patiently wait to feel the Divine Presence.[13]

This very gentle approach depends largely on an intellectual concept, i.e., "consider yourself" or think of or picture yourself in the divine presence. Then you set your mind in a certain way. Control your thoughts and wait upon God.

Our inward turning is most likely to occur to us if we have maintained or can recover our "original simplicity," that is, a childlike spirit marked by an almost naïve belief. Perhaps "naïve" is not the best descriptive word. But the idea is of a condition approaching "absolute trust" in the faithfulness of God, total dedication to Christ in perpetual surrender to His will and obedience to His voice conveyed to us through both the written word and consolations of the Holy Spirit. As we walk in this daily surrender to Him, accepting His will for us in place of ours, often in repudiating our own reason and understanding and in opposition to the actual conditions of our lives which are blatantly obvious, we choose trust in Him over empirical evidence, we find intense consolation of the Spirit and enhanced assurances accompany us along the way.

For many of us, this was the mark of our original entrance into believing faith. These were the characteristics of "the Hour I first believed" as the line from the beloved hymn "Amazing Grace"[14] terms that high phase of our experience. We may remember the high glory of our first

12. Ibid.

13. *A Guide to True Peace* (Harper & Bros, nd), 24–25

14. John Newton, *The Baptist Hymnal*, 330.

days with Christ. We remember the "Floods of Joy o'er my soul like the sea billows roll, Since Jesus came into my heart."[15]

Those pure, clear, decisive moments return with pristine clarity. "The hour I first believed" contained all the spiritual possibilities that would be unfolded to us. Embracing the One who has embraced us is a reenactment of that glorious occasion when we first accepted Him as Lord and Savior. Subsequent spiritual experience, which may seem higher, more complete, more transcendent, more glorious is in fact a reappearance of the wonderful directness and immeasurable sweetness of that one to one encounter with the Living God and Savior.

---

15. Rufus H. McDaniel, "Since Jesus Came Into My Heart," *The Baptist Hymnal*, 441.

14

Referring Everything to God

THE BIBLE IS VERY specific on this point, urging the act of ". . . casting all your care upon him;"[1] We must refer every aspect of our experience to the Lord. We must cast every element of our experience on Him ". . . for he careth for you."[2] Isaiah states that the "Suffering Servant," the coming Messiah

> . . . was wounded for our transgressions, he was bruised for our iniquities: the chastisement of our peace was upon him: and with his stripes we are healed. All we like sheep have gone astray; we have turned every one to his own way; and the Lord hath laid on him the iniquity of us all.[3]

In the Gospel of Matthew the evangelist paraphrases Isaiah as follows: ". . . Himself took our infirmities, and bare our sicknesses."[4] Because God cares for us He has already born our troubles and cares, our sicknesses and infirmities. Jesus Christ has already suffered for us. He has born our sufferings and griefs. Why then should we bear what He has already born? Why should we carry what He has already carried? Why should we endure what He has already endured. The answer of course is obvious. We should not bear them. We should refer them to the One who has already suffered for them. We should cast them on the One who has paid the penalty for them. We should take them to the One who invites us to do so.

We are to take all our burdens to the Lord and leave them there. He has provided a way to relieve the inward distress of the soul so that full and complete fellowship with Him can be achieved within the sacred

1. First Peter 5:7.
2. Ibid.
3. Isaiah 53:5–6.
4. Matthew 8:17b.

room, that is, the inner recesses of the soul, the temple in the heart, the Holy of Holies in the heart. When we have cast all our care on the Lord, the sacred room is cleansed. This allows us to come to Him in a more complete and intense way as hindrances and blockages are removed.

We are to refer *all* our care, concern, sickness, injury, grief, emotional distress, trouble, mental disturbance, loneliness, anger, lust, despair, depression, and of course, sin, as well as everything else to God.

Everything! Everything is to be referred to the Lord: imagination run amok, unwanted and repulsive thoughts that run uncontrollably through the mind, neurosis, shyness, shame, embarrassment, results of a deprived childhood, and all other conditions imaginable and those beyond our knowledge. Yes, even the subconscious content of our psyche, things of which we are not even aware, things which are buried deep below our consciousness, repressed memories, covered up injuries, denied anger, unacknowledged rage—all these and every other aspect of our experience are to be referred to God.

This invitation to refer everything to God includes joyous occasions as well as the sad ones. It applies to the happy events that also mark our lives. The days of sunshine; the moon-lit nights. The great moments, the significant occasions, the music and the celebrations, the times when we feel the glory of an eternal impulse radiating through our hearts. All these are to be referred to the Lord:

1. A conviction, a divine visitation, a sweet voice calling;
2. A moment of moral clarity, rational insight, an opened understanding;
3. Sunshine, laughter, the warmth of love, family occasions;
4. Days of grace;
5. A new born child, the simple innocence of children;
6. Moments of well-being, sensations of wholeness and integration.

The thousand joys that mark our lives are to be referred to God also. Cast them upon the Lord. Take these great occasions to the Lord and leave them there also.

When we refer everything to the Lord, we will be living and moving and having our being in Christ. We will be in Christ and Christ will be in us! The temple of the Holy Spirit in our hearts will radiate with heavenly light and the sound of angel's choruses will resound in our spiritual ears.

We will walk in the light. We will have restored unto us the joy of our salvation. A right spirit and a happy heart will be our heritage and our daily endowment.

So cast everything on the Lord. Refer everything to God. Ground your daily experience in the Eternal. Then you will hear the small still voice clearly and distinctly.

The music of the spheres will resound through your soul. Christ will be your All in All.

This is God's will for you and for me—that we should refer our total experience to Him; the negative, destructive and painful and also the joyous, the triumphant, the daily glories that attend our way. We can begin to do this now! Because the Great Physician now is near, the sympathizing Jesus as the hymn writer put it.[5] He is physician, psychiatrist and "Wonderful Counselor."[6] Compassion for people is a constant theme in Jesus ministry. He often intervened into people's situations and performed miraculous works from the restoring of Lazarus and others from the dead, rescuing madmen from self-destructive actions, cleansing lepers, restoring sight to the blind, confronting spiritual and psychological problems, and all manner of deliverances, great and small.

Since His success on the cross and in the resurrection He is all the more willing and able to help us. So we must cast all our cares on Him; referring every concern, care, victory, triumph, attitude and state of mind to Him for His therapeutic applications.

How brilliantly Shakespeare described the ideal physician. MacBeth calls in the physician and proposes the treatment he thinks is needed for his ailing and disturbed wife. She is racked by guilt and anxiety over the crimes she and her husband have committed. So MacBeth asks of the doctor:

> Cure her of that.
> Canst thou not minister to a mind diseased,
> Pluck from the memory of a rooted sorrow,
> Raze out the written troubles of the brain,
> And with some sweet oblivious antidote
> Cleanse the stuff'd bosom of that perilous stuff
> Which weighs upon the heart?[7]

---

5. William Hunter. "The Great Physician." The Baptist Hymnal, 188.

6. Isaiah 9:6b.

7. "MacBeth" Act V, Sc. iii.

What an insightful description of the ideal treatment for all manner of disease. Jesus certainly exemplifies the ideal physician. He can do all these things. He opens the center of the soul to us where healing and wholeness are readily available. In His capacity as the eternal *Logos*, He first grants us existence as human and then offers us grace and glory, salvation and sanctity, emotional stability, and bodily health.

So Jesus has done a lot more than practice medicine and the general healing arts. The scripture tells us that He has "born our sorrows and carried our griefs." In His own body He has born every sin and ailment that so easily beset us. Jesus is the owner of all the troubles we are carrying around. He simply asks that we give them to Him, their true owner. There is nothing we suffer that Jesus has not already suffered, worked through, and provided the cure.

So these are things are not ours. They are intruders into our lives. It is therefore a foolish act for us to bear them again; to carry them around as if they were ours. It is an act of selfishness for us to carry griefs and sorrows which are not ours, but His. It is sinful for us to selfishly grasp them, to assume possession of them, and to assert ownership over them. So we are asked to refer them to Him; we are to cast all our cares upon Him.

Just as Jesus cleansed the Temple in Jerusalem, so must we cleanse the temple of the heart. If the heart is emptied of all these disturbances, distractions and blockages, Jesus will come in and we will enter our own hearts to be with Him. Jesus overturned the tables of the merchandisers and cast them out of God's Temple, which they had made into a place of commerce. Although many techniques might be used by us to cleanse our inner temple, such as prayer and devotion, visualizing the actual carrying them to Jesus on the Cross, or transferring them spiritually to the indwelling Christ, or simply confessing that since He is the final ground of all our experience, everything that happens to us happens to Him.[8] They are already His which we can recognize in an act of spiritual release. But the nearest thing available to us that resembles Jesus' aggressive act of cleansing the Temple is the act of repentance. Repentance breaks the hold of sin and guilt, expels the intrusive reign of sin and death, sickness and infirmity, and sets our feet on higher ground, allowing us to start over with a clean slate. Then we are to repent of being sick? Are we to repent of being depressed? We are to repent of being rejected and lonely? If we have not consciously referred all these to Him, the answer must be a decisive *Yes.*

8. Matthew 25:31–45.

15

Consecrating Our Cares

IF THE LORD SHOULD choose not to accept our effort to cast our cares, burdens and sicknesses on Him, something different is required of us. If, in His wisdom and compassion, He chooses to allow our distress to continue, then we must embrace them as God's will. This different strategy is to accept them as an act of faith which then allows God to consecrate them to His own service and purpose. Either God will remove our burdens or He will consecrate them as instruments for His own use. One of these two possibilities will occur. Our prayer of upward casting should be "Heal me, O Lord or consecrate my trouble as instruments in your hands!"

Until we have attempted to cast our cares on Him, we are bearing our troubles in a sinful manner. That is, we are either demonstrating that we are ignorant of the healing aspect of the sacrifice Jesus made on the cross, or we believe that God has sent us these burdens, or we lack the faith to attempt to place our cares on Jesus, or we are too indolent to make the effort, or we think that there is some discipline or judgment being accomplished by our condition. Failure to cast our cares on Him is an implicit denial of the healing power of Jesus and transforms our sickness into sin.

In attempting to cast all our burdens on Him, we are recognizing the monumental truth that Jesus has born our griefs, carried our sorrows, and paid the penalty in His own body and soul on Calvary's cross. By casting our burdens on Him, we are acknowledging that He has formally freed us from all our infirmities and that we are seeking to actualize that result.

In the action we are discussing, what is accomplished is that sickness, suffering and grief are transposed to a higher spiritual level. In the very act, whether it results in the reversal or remission of our problems, whether physical or psychological, we are entering the realm of the eternal will and purpose of God. Success does not necessarily imply that our problems are solved, or that our infirmities are removed. The very act of casting them on the Lord transforms them to an entirely different kind of entity. It transforms them into spiritual problems and therefore now capable of spiritual solutions.

Until we have presented our burdens to the Lord, it is not appropriate for us to bear them. That is, we are sinfully accepting them as an inevitable condition about which we can do nothing. This is a reasonable statement of the situation—here we are sick, weary, depressed, disabled, and yet there is the solution. Christ has born our sorrows and grief. He has paid the price by suffering to achieve full redemption for us. All we have to do is to apply to Him: to present our situation to Him for His gracious solution. But we have not done so. Therefore it is a sin for us to be sick. It is a sin for us to be weary, depressed or disabled. It is a sin for the simple reason that there is a divine solution. But we have not asked for the solution. We have not cast our cares on Him. So we bear them without good reason, without necessity, without divine approval.

Then we present them to God. We cast all our cares on him in accordance with the scripture. He could very well heal us totally. The solution has already been achieved on the cross by Christ. There is no hindrance to the solution. Christ has died for us and we have all healing available through His redemptive action. We may cast them on Him but He seems to do nothing about them, then what? Perhaps we have presented them to Him and yet they continue to reside in us. We continue to be sick, injured, grief stricken, depressed, depleted, and exhausted, what shall we say? Under those circumstances, we must come to understand that God's solution was not to remove them, but rather to consecrate them; to make them holy; to incorporate them into His plans and purposes; to make them useful instruments of His. They become mediators of His grace. They become therapeutic devices for ourselves and for others. They are instruments of His peace; channels of blessing to ourselves and those around us.

Consecration is one of the two alternatives in our casting all our cares on Him. Consecration is as valid a solution as the removal of our problems. If God chooses to leave the problem in place, allowing it to continue in our lives, then He consecrates it, making it a useful condition through which blessings may flow and by means of which we may show forth His glory. Whatever He does not remove, He consecrates, transforms, makes holy, adopts as an instrument of His will and purpose.

The dynamics of this consecration leads us to the highest understanding of Jesus' participation in our lives, His sharing in our experience and indwelling in our hearts. If God in His grace decides that He will not remove the burden from us, He has in effect decided that Jesus will not "bear the cross alone." God has decided that you or I, the sick, suffering one, will bear the burden but that Jesus will bear it with us. This is the most intense fellowship; the holiest of all interactions between Christ and ourselves. If God had removed our burden, then Jesus would be bearing it alone. By leaving it in us and on us, we become sharers with Christ, participating in the power of His resurrection and the fellowship of His suffering.

There are just two alternatives: we will either be relieved of our care, or we will have it consecrated. What we must not do is carry around unconsecrated sickness, grief, distress, disturbance, disruption, injury, infirmity, brokenness, fragmentation of soul, and depletion of spirit. We must do one of two things—receive the healing from the cross by referring it to its rightful domain or receive consecration of the care in the act of presenting it to Christ. In short, whatever our problem or care may be, we must either get it removed or get it consecrated just as Paul received divine assurance concerning his thorn in the flesh: ". . . My grace is sufficient for thee: for my strength is made perfect in weakness."[1]

Removal or inundation in sufficient grace—these are the possible results of the spiritual act of "casting all our care on him" for He truly "careth for you."

---

1. Second Corinthians 12:9a.

16

The Holy Spirit in the Depths

THE HOLY SPIRIT WORKS in our subconscious selves in one of two ways: secretly and without our knowledge until the work becomes an accomplished fact, or openly with our full participation as the Spirit brings the stored material to the level of conscious awareness. The difference in this and the bringing of insight to awareness in classical psychoanalysis is that the Spirit selects the material that should be brought to awareness rather than the random choice of memory. This selection by the Spirit occurs through a comprehensive process of intense searching. Knowing the human psyche and understanding the problem and its source, the Spirit works with the material that is causing the most urgent problem in the person's life.

The Apostle Paul refers to the work of the Spirit which suggests what is said above and gives some Biblical justification for the claim:

> LIKEWISE the Spirit also helpeth our infirmities: for we know not what we should pray for as we ought; but the Spirit itself maketh intercession for us with groanings which cannot be uttered. And he that searcheth the hearts knoweth what is the mind of the Spirit, because he maketh intercession for the saints according to the will of God.[1]

In the wisdom of God, the Spirit selects the material to be brought up and dealt with. That choice is beyond human ability. We don't know what we should ask for because we don't know what is there within our hidden depths and furthermore if we did know, we would not know which segment of our experience was causing the trouble. It is a divine process which produces a divine result.

---

1. Romans 8:26–27.

When the Spirit is working at this level, our conscious participation is required. We deliberately and urgently ask the Spirit to search our depths. We pray for Him to probe, discover and illuminate the block of experience that is the source of our problem. We may say:

> O Holy Spirit! Please search the secret recesses of my soul. Discover the experience now preserved there which is the source of my trouble. Find the fragment of my life stored there which is causing me such distress.
>
> O Lord, lead me to rightmindedness and peace. Disclose unto me through your infinite wisdom and your knowledge of the mind of God and my own disturbed soul where my problem lies. Shine your holy light upon the source of my unrest and enable me to overcome the emotional pain that so tortures me now. Then, O Lord, enable me to deal with my past experience in such a way that I may find relief and deliverance. Give me the ability to refer this and all things to God, in whose name I pray. Amen.

We must come to know, recall, acknowledge, confess, agonize over, and analyze that which the Spirit brings to our awareness. We are depending on the Holy Spirit's knowledge of the structure of the self and the dynamics of healing that is called for. Our own ability to make the right choice of the material is put aside. But once the material is brought to our awareness, we are active participants as we interact with it once again. After we have properly processed it, then we upwardly level it to God, that is we "cast it on Him;" we refer it to Him.

After the material has been brought to our awareness, then we may deal with it according to the techniques of therapy to which we have been lead in communion with the Spirit in the attitude of prayer. But the ultimate solution depends on our successful referring it to God. We may have undergone painful processes as this material is renewed in our consciousness. We have been called on to wrestle with it, to own it, to repent of it, to honestly acknowledge it. But now the victory, described so well with interesting imagery by John Welch:

> Somewhere, deep down, a healing process begins which slowly mends the shattered psyche and gives strength for renewed living. The source of healing is a mystery. But we know that a door has opened where we thought only a wall existed.[2]

---

2. John Welch, *Spiritual Pilgrims* (New York: Paulist Press. 1982), 136.

The second manner in which the Spirit may deal with our problem is similar to the first. Of course, it is the Spirit Himself who chooses which way He will accomplish his work. We may ask Him in prayer to search our hearts and heal our injuries. Now He enters our depths and searches as in the first method. The difference here is that our conscious participation is not required. In this case, we do not know what the problem is. We know that something is disturbing our serenity and well-being. Without identifying the problem, the Spirit begins to work, locating the problem and devises the healing process. The Spirit does it all. That is, He does not bring the troublesome material to our awareness. He searches into the deeps and finds the source of our distress and simply refers it to God on His own and we are not required to go through the stages of acknowledging, confessing, agonizing over, and referring it to God. The sought after healing is presented to us as an accomplished fact. We have asked Him for help and He has given it to us without any effort on our part. We may never know what the problem was, but now we feel a sense of release and wholeness that we had never felt before.

A slight variation on this second method is this: He works in us while we are completely unaware that He is doing so. We have not asked specifically. We have not prayed for His help. No doubt, He has responded to some need which we did not know about. We had not recognized the problem that was detrimental to us. So without our asking and without our knowledge, the Spirit enters our depths, finds the problems, solves it by referring the troublesome material to God. We have not been conscious of what He was actually doing. We may experience a strange sense of comfort and well-being. We may experience a new sense of expectation as if something great was about to happen to us. But we do not know what is happening. We feel exuberant and exhilarated as we sense that great things are happening to us and in us. And suddenly, there is! Healing and wholeness presented to us as a *fait accompli*. In a "brief, bright moment" we receive a silent testimony that some wonderful spiritual deliverance has been granted to us.

In this instance, the Spirit may choose to keep His participation in our inner lives completely secret. He may not give us the slightest inkling of the great process going on within us. We may have no indication at all of the healing and reconstruction of our inner life that is going on until it is completely finished. Then it is presented as an accomplished fact and we didn't even know it was in progress! No evidence has been given—not even the feelings of exhilaration or elevation. No sense of mystery. No warming of the heart. No sense of excitement or well-being. The Spirit chose for his own reasons to keep it all from us until it was finished. Deep within the psyche or soul, a door has opened and deliverance and victory have stepped forth. Deep with in the deepest self completely without our knowledge or participation, the unbelievable has occurred. We have been made whole.

Such spiritual healing is sometimes attributed to natural processes. "We just got over it," we may say. While there are extremely powerful healing agencies and processes in nature, disruptions in the deep self require the unique therapy that only the Holy Spirit can give.

17

Pray Without Ceasing

OUR SOULS ARE MADE for constant, unceasing prayer. Everything we say, we say before God. Everything we think, we think before God. Everything we feel, we feel before God. He is a party to our every thought and word. The entire content of our mental and emotional life, as well as our active life, is always occurring in the presence of the Divine. Therefore, since our total consciousness is instantly before God, our entire activity—thought, acts and words—can become prayer. In this way, we can fulfill the sometimes perplexing admonition to "Pray without ceasing."[1]

Many efforts have been made to show how we can fulfill the goal of unceasing prayer. For instance, the Jesus Prayer of the Eastern Orthodox Church tradition is an attempt to practice constant prayer using actual words either spoken or thought. The contemplative infused prayer of the Western Church tradition is also an attempt to fulfill this requirement of constancy of prayer. If we recognize however that our entire mental life is ever before God, that all of our thoughts and feelings as well as our actions, are a part of God's own experience, we can turn our whole souls to the service of adoration and praise. That is, our entire conscious life can become prayer to God.

Therefore, let our thoughts often be thoughts about God, filled with acclamation and praise.

Let our yearning be yearning for God.

Let gratitude and thanksgiving mount up on the wings of all our mental and psychic functions as they are constantly coming before the throne of grace!

---

1. First Thessalonians 5:17.

Let repentance for our sins be offered to Him through our broken and contrite hearts as godly sorrow for our failings and shortcomings wafts upward into His presence.

Let forgiveness of others be a constant state of mind for us as God observes our relations with our neighbors, friends, family members, and acquaintances and happily accepts and approves.

Let us bless others with positive affirmations of their worth and wishes for their well-being since God takes notice and accepts on our efforts as prayer.

Our entire mental life, then, can be carried on with awareness that ultimately God is the subject and recipient of all our mental and emotional experience. Take television or radio broadcasting as an example. The signal goes forth constantly. As a science, broadcasting is neutral in itself. It simply utilizes the processes contained in the natural world. But the quality of the programming can be varied. It can be positive or negative, useful or totally frivolous. That's the way it is with our psychic life. Thoughts, ideas, feelings impressions, reactions form a steady and automatic flow of data. This material is constantly emanating and entering the world. It instantly comes before God and enters into His experience. By making sure that the content of this constant stream of experience that flows from our souls is positive, affirmative, celebratory, joyous, filled with thanksgiving and praise, forgivness, oriented toward repentance, filled with faith, expressing a sense of trust and dependence on God, looking to Him for our "supply," and containing openness and receptivity to His grace and salvation, we make our total experience an operative prayer.

These elements of our inner lives, which are always before God, become the fulfillment of the vision of Paul that we should "Pray without ceasing." By changing the content of our inner processes and the objectives of our outer action, our lives become truly lives of prayer. When we convert these automatic processes into unceasing prayers, the life of our soul becomes a bold and constant stance before God, one which He approves, in which He is glorified, one which He will bless and reward.

18

The Unsleeping Heart

"**I** SLEEP, BUT MY heart awaketh."[1] Or as this verse is translated in more modern terms in the Revised Standard Version as "I slept but my heart was awake."[2] Because of the miraculous way we are created, with amazing physical and psychological faculties, inward prayer can be accomplished even when the body is fast asleep. In the Song of Solomon, the heart is kept awake by the intensity of the writer's feeling for "the Beloved." But more comprehensively, we know that, even in the deepest sleep, the "heart" is awake all through the night.

This constant wakefulness of the heart testifies to the nature of the creative activity of God that brought us into existence as living souls. A part of us is like God, whose very life/spirit/breath is the basis of our existence as human beings. For God Himself is always awake. As the Psalmist says: "Behold, he that keepeth Israel shall neither slumber nor sleep."[3] Indeed as the Old Testament writer said, ". . . the eyes of the Lord run to and fro throughout the whole earth . . ."[4] Since we are created in the image of God, it is appropriate that there is a part of us that is always aware, always awake. The fact that the "heart" never sleeps reflects this image of God in us. The eternal awakeness of God is replicated in Solomon's observation that "I slept but my heart was awake."[5]

There is a great spiritual resource, a rich stream of constant blessing and spiritual growth in this activity of the heart during times of sleep.

---

1. Song of Solomon 5:2.
2. Ibid., RSV.
3. Psalm 121:4.
4. Second Chronicles 16:9a.
5. Song of Soloman 5:2, RSV.

This capacity of the heart can be utilized to fulfill the admonition of the Apostle Paul to "pray without ceasing."[6]

The Psalm writer may have experienced a nocturnal deliverance when he wrote these words: "For his anger endureth but a moment; in his favor is life: weeping may endure for a night, but joy cometh in the morning."[7] In the night, during his sleep, the Psalmist's heart had found its peace with God. He may have wept while awake or even during sleep. But in the stillness of the night while his body was in repose, his soul had found its rest in God through the deep communion with its Creator and Father.

Although not referring to inward prayer, Moses assured the Israelites that ". . . in the morning, then ye shall see the glory of the Lord."[8] Shakespeare spoke of the ". . . Sleep that knits up the ravell'd sleave of care."[9] It is not going too far to believe that the restoration of spirit, the renewal of the joy of God's salvation, the healing of the body of injury and disease, the deepening of resolve and commitment as well as other spiritual values have been accomplished through the secret prayer of the heart during the night while we were fast asleep. It is unlikely that the heart is idle. In its time of freedom from the interests of the mind and the constraints of the body, the heart traverses the universe. Surely it naturally soars upward to its maker and source to engage in renewing and recreating communion with the One from whom it came.

Further indication that the heart is spiritually active during sleep is the fact that in the Bible God often communicates His will to certain of His chosen through dreams. The instances of this are numerous and one need only to consult the Bible for examples. Jacob, Zechariah, Joseph and many others received God's revelation through the active reception of the heart during sleep. Who knows what great things may come to us in the night; who knows what God may say to us tonight while we are asleep while our hearts remain awake, open, receptive? The heart is a spiritual receptor and a proactive faculty for spiritual advance as it remains alert, conscious, and receptive during periods of sleep.

The heart may be more productive in terms of inward prayer if specific data is placed before it. This should be in the form of a suggestion

6. First Thessalonians 5:17.

7. Psalm 30:5.

8. Exodus 16:7a.

9. *The Tragedy of MacBeth* Act II, Sc. II.

rather than a command. We may suggest to our hearts something along these lines—ask your heart to probe your depths and present to God your unconscious needs and to seek forgiveness for your secret sins or seek a remedy for your hidden faults. Just before falling asleep, you may say to your heart: "Consider this problem tonight;" naming it specifically. Ask it to work out a solution to some troubling situation before morning. Define it concretely. Implore it to find a way through a named problem during this time of sleep. Petition your heart to discover an open door leading through the dilemma you are now facing. Ask it to heal anger, grief, insecurity, and anxiety. Be very specific in the description of the problem in question as well as the result you desire to be accomplished.

When the heart is guided by gentle suggestions like this, we can count on some definite solutions being reached. We can look forward to progress being made. Of course, faith is the operative state of mind that will bring about the victory. If we believe that God is going to work through our psyche during the night to accomplish what He wills to do, this faith secures the possibility. This is not very different from any other spiritual activity. Everything involving God is based on faith and trust.

When we awake refreshed, aware of some victory, then we can rejoice at the effectiveness of inward prayer accomplished by the unsleeping heart. When we can say in the morning, "I am no longer angry over certain slights, insults or injuries inflicted by others, I have forgiven everyone involved," the slate is wiped clean. Then we know a victory has been won. Or when my mind held a thousand opinions when I went to sleep but now when I awake, I have singleness of mind, a commitment to a course of action, a certainty of direction and my faculties are fully focused, my heart has accomplished a great purpose during the night. I celebrate its ministry of inward prayer. If I could not feel assured of forgiveness or even of salvation on going to sleep but in the morning I feel at one with God, renewed in the joy of His salvation, there is cause for rejoicing. When my feet seemed to mire into the sands of weakness last night, but now in the morning I am aware of standing on the Rock that does not move, I am thereby blessed when the promise is fulfilled for me: "And in the morning, . . . ye shall see the glory of the Lord;"[10]

---

10. Exodus 16:7a.

19

Short But Ardent Prayers

THE ANONYMOUS AUTHOR OF *The Cloud of Unknowing* refers to short, spontaneous prayers as "piercing heaven."[1] This author affirms that the shorter the better. Indeed, if such prayers can be kept to a single word, that would be preferable. Spontaneous prayers which ". . . rise evermore suddenly unto God, without any means or any premeditation in special coming before, or going therewith."[2] Even better the single word should be a single syllable. If one cries "fire," he has had no time to think about his cry or prepare his announcement and

> . . . this little word 'fire' stirreth rather and pierceth more hastily the ears of his hearers, so doth a little word of one syllable when it is not only spoken or thought, but privily meant in the deepness of spirit. . . . it pierceth the ears of Almighty God than doth any long psalter unmindfully mumbled in the teeth. And therefore it is written, that short prayer pierceth heaven."[3]

Francis DeSales recommends that one should get in the habit of offering short, ardent prayers throughout the day or night, while at work or play. These do not have to be spoken if the situation is not conducive to spoken prayer.

DeSales recommends to his correspondent: "Aspire, then, very often to God, Philothia, by short but ardent movements of your heart."[4] Short, ardent and piercing, these brief prayers, perhaps no more than one

1. Evelyn Underhill, ed., *A Book of Contemplation The Which Is Called The Cloud of Unknowing, In The Which A Soul Is Oned With God*, (London: John M. Watkins 1950), chapter 37.

2. Ibid.

3. Ibid.

4. *Introduction to the Devout Life* ch 19 (London: Burns, Oates and Washburn, 1924).

sentence, or perhaps only an ejaculatory affirmation, a word or phrase, emerging from a true heart will conduct us into the presence of God.

Then Saint Francis DeSales suggests categories of these "short but ardent movements" of the heart toward God. The subject matter of these might be one or more of the following:[5]

1. admire his heaven

2. invoke his help

3. cast yourself in spirit at the foot of the cross

4. adore his goodness

5. speak to him frequently about your salvation

6. give him your heart a thousand times a day

7. fix your interior eyes upon his sweetness

8. give your hand to him as a child to father

9. put him on your breast as a delicious nosegay

10. plant him in your soul as a standard

11. make a thousand different movements of your heart to give yourself the love of God, and to excite yourself to a passionate and tender love of this divine Spouse.

This kind of prayer can be useful in conducting us to the throne of grace from which God rules in the "highest heaven." When we upwardly level our cares and concerns, the heart is unburdened and the divine interest is engaged. And it can be a significant help to us in drawing near to Him in His dwelling place within our hearts which have become "broken and contrite," by the conviction and godly sorrow which have lead to faith by means of which He dwells within us.

DeSales summarizes the value of this kind of spontaneous prayer:

> . . . our soul in giving itself to secret and familiar intercourse with God, will become all perfumed with his perfections; and, moreover, this exercise is not difficult, for it can be interwoven with all our own affairs and occupations, without any detriment to them whatsoever; inasmuch as, both in spiritual retirement, and in these interior movements, we only make little and short digres-

5. Ibid.

sions which do not hinder us in any way, but greatly help us to carry out whatever we are doing.[6]

These short spontaneous prayers woven into our daily lives, whether we are at work or at rest, are indispensable to the development of the contemplative, spiritual life. This practice, DeSales urges, should be embraced "with your whole heart"[7] and never abandoned.

These kinds of spontaneous, piercing prayers interspersed into all our activities will bring us closer to the center of our own selves. As Meister Eckerd has so perceptively remarked, ". . . it is we ourselves who are absent"[8] from our own selves, and not God who is always present to the soul. This kind of prayer will help conduct us to the door of the sacred precinct of the heart. And as we draw near to that holy space within us, God who is within will perhaps open the door of it to us as we approach Him in this manner.

6. DeSales ch. 13.

7. Ibid.

8. Blakney 132.

20

The Jesus Prayer

SOMETIMES OUR CAPACITY TO enter the throne room seems impaired. Even our interest in doing so may have been reduced by sin or dissipated by troubles retained, that is, not cast on the Lord. Our ability to present ourselves to God at the center of our own self seems to have totally left us and we are incapable of entering the sacred room. Psychological overcrowdedness, emotional scatteredness, disintegration, and distraction have taken us far away from the sweet serenity, the holy beauty, the luminous power, and gracious creativeness of the sacred center.

Although we must not become terrified at this condition, we must soon correct it and resume life at the center, entering His presence again with thanksgiving and praise. In the meantime, we continue external praise and prayer, worship and obedience which are rendered to God as His due. All the while, however, we know we are not living at the center and we long to soon reenter the sacred room.

When we have continued in this condition sufficiently long to receive the benefits and values God is showing us through it, we may take deliberate action to reenter the elevated life at the sacred center. The "Jesus Prayer" or "Prayer of the Heart" of Eastern Orthodox Christianity may be of great help to us in this regard.

This prayer was practiced from the middle of the fifth century and passed by word of mouth and from teacher to pupil in spiritual direction. In the eleventh century, written reference to it is made by St. Symeon the New Theologian.[1]

> Later it was the subject of special treatises Nicephorus the Monk (thirteenth century), and above all by St. Gregory of Sinai, who at

---

1. Vladimir Lossky, *The Mystical Theology of the Eastern Church* (Crestwood, New York: St. Vladimir's Seminary Press, 1976), 209.

the beginning of the fourteenth century re-established its practice on Mount Athos.[2]

Under the monks of Mount Athos in Macedonia, this method of prayer known as *Hesychasm* (from the Greek word meaning "stillness") became a practice of inner stillness and concentration before the divine presence.[3] At first the prayer consisted of voluminous repetition of the name of Jesus. Later, it was expanded into a somewhat longer, yet still brief, form. This prayer has become a valuable spiritual resource in Orthodox Christianity and the Russian religious philosopher, Nicholas Berdyaev has said that it "lies at the very heart of Orthodox mysticism."[4]

It was believed that the name of Jesus contained within it the total divine energy. Constant repetition of the name brought this presence of God into action through which it penetrated the souls of the one repeating the name "Jesus, Jesus, Jesus" thousands and thousands of times. The little book, *The Way of a Pilgrim*, tells the story of one man's experience in the practice of this prayer.[5]

After a while, the prayer produces the experience of ecstasy culminating in a beholding of the heavenly Light. Gregory Palamas taught that in repeating the Jesus Prayer a man was performing the highest act for which he was created, exulting in the light of the Transfiguration which shone in and through Jesus on Mount Tabor.[6]

In due time, the Jesus Prayer or Prayer of the Heart took on a more extended form. Originally, it was formulated, "Lord Jesus Christ, Son of God, have mercy on me." Later, seeming to incorporate the publican's prayer in Jesus' parable, "God be merciful to me a sinner,"[7] it became fixed as follows: "Lord Jesus Christ, Son of God, have mercy on me, a sinner."[8]

Coordinated with the process of breathing, one should say while inhaling, "Lord Jesus Christ, Son of God" and add the phrase, "have mercy on me, a sinner" while exhaling. Aligning the words with one's breathing

---

2. Lossky 209–10.

3. Sidney Spencer, *Mysticism in World Religion* (South Brunswick New York: A. S. Barnes & Co. 1963), 228.

4. Cited in Spencer, 228.

5. Tran. R. M. French (New York: Ballentine Books, 1974).

6. Spencer, 228.

7. Luke 28:13b.

8. Timothy Ware, *The Orthodox Church* (London: Penguin Books, 1991), 74–75.

seems to add to the prayer's power to produce elevated feelings of ecstasy which opens the sacred room, or center of the soul.

Recognizing that no mere mechanical method will lead us into the sacred room, we need not fear that we are intruders, such as Jesus referred to concerning "those that come in by some other way" and therefore are trespassers into the heavenly realm. God would not admit us by means of any inferior or underhanded ways. So when we gain entrance, regardless of the means, our entering will be in accordance with His will and therefore valid and spiritual. Entrance into the divine presence is always a gift of God. Any practice of prayer that lifts us up to the door through which we may gain access to God's presence is not to be depreciated. The Jesus Prayer has proven its effectiveness over and over again for many seekers. It is especially useful when our minds are so confused that we cannot formulate an acceptable prayer and our souls are so confused that we truly "do not know what we should pray for."

21

The Single Eye and the Power of Intention

ONE THING WE CAN do to vitalize our faith is to develop the proper intention. If we are to come into His presence within the sacred room we must intend to do so. We must intend to please Him; intend to find Him, intend to behold Him with the inner vision. Jesus referred to the importance of intention when He said, ". . . if . . . thine eye be single, thy whole body will be full of light."[1] Jesus means that we should not be "double minded" or hold conflicting loyalties, or attempt to serve two masters. He makes the bold claim that if we are focused on one thing then we will have fullness of light. That makes it an easy choice to be singleminded in all aspects of our life. Fullness of light is readily available and attainable with limited effort.

Jan Van Ruysbroek (1293–1381) defines the single intention in this way: "That intention is single which intends nothing but God and all things as they exist with respect to God."[2] He continues to commend and recommend the single intention as the answer to all manner of spiritual problems. He states:

> Every single good work, however small it may be, which is offered up to God with love and with an honest and single intention, earns for us a greater likeness to Him and eternal life in Him. The single intention draws together our dissipated powers in unity of the spirit, and impels the spirit on its way toward God. The single intention is the end and the beginning and the adornment of all virtues. The single intention offers to God praise and honor and all

1. Matthew 6:22.

2. Jan Van Ruysbroek, *The Spiritual Espousals* ch. 49, trans. Eric Colledge, (New York: Harper & Bros., nd).

virtues, and it surpasses and transcends itself and all the heavens and all things, and it finds God in the single foundation of itself.[3]

Calling the single intent "the foundation of all spirituality," Ruysbroek points to its centering and unifying power:

> The single intent drives out dissimulation and duplicity, and man shall keep it and exercise it in all his works above all things. For it keeps man continually before God, clear in understanding, zealous in virtues and free from fear, both here and in the day of judgment."[4]

Clearly, we will wish to utilize such a powerful technique in our coming to the One who is always there in the sacred room. Other spiritual masters have also strongly commended the role and power of the single intent. William Law (1686-1761) states that all spiritual and moral failure is due to the absence of simple intention. Law says:

> . . . if you will stop here and ask yourself, why you are not so devoted as the primitive Christians, your heart will tell you that it is neither through ignorance nor inability but purely because you never thoroughly intended it.[5]

According to Law this "intention to please God" will bring about a reform of personal piety, cleaning up the character by expurgating offensive habits: "Let a man but have so much piety as to intend to please God in all the actions of his life and then he will swear no more."[6] Sincere intention would change "the face of the world" and make "true piety and exemplary holiness . . . as common and visible as buying and selling or any trade in life."[7]

A popular English psychic healer of recent date has commented revealingly on the power of intention in non-medical healing. When asked about the proper technique for accomplishing psychic healing, Harry Edwards said, "They (healings) may take place under any kind of technique which has a sincere healing intention as its source. If the intention

3. Ibid., 149, 49.

4. op.cit.

5. *A Serious Call to a Devout and Holy Life*, (Philadelphia: Westminster Press, 1955), 21.

6. Ibid., 21.

7. Ibid., 22.

is to seek healing, then it will take place in spite of whatever the healer or person does."[8]

A more recent philosopher-theologian, the Danish thinker of great influence, Soren Kierkegaard, referred to the ability "to will one thing" as the source personal unity and psychological integration which produces "purity of heart." "To will one thing" is what the older classical devotional writers called "the single intent." Kierkegaard celebrates the power of willing one thing in a beautiful prayer-litany at the beginning of his book in which he asks for the ability to so will:

> In prosperity may Thou grant perseverance to will one thing; amid distractions, collectedness to will one thing; in suffering, patience to will one thing. Oh, Thou that giveth both the beginning and the completion, may Thou early, at the dawn of day, give to the young man the resolution to will one thing. As the day wanes, may Thou give to the old man a renewed remembrance of his first resolution, that the first may be like the last, the last like the first, in possession of a life that has willed only one thing.[9]

Kierkegaard goes on to lament that sin has hindered us in our willing one thing. "Delay, blockage, interruption, delusion and corruption" have all had their say in our ability to will the one thing. The effect of repentance is the restoration of the original ability as he requests of God that He might "give the courage once again to will one thing."[10]

The "one thing" to be willed is God: "Thee the One" as Kierkegaard describes Him. Willing this one thing, or in other terms, having a single intent, is seen as the source of spiritual unity and Christian victory.

8. Paris Flammonde, *The Mystic Healers*, (New York: Stein & Day, 1974), 156.

9. Glasgow, *Purity of Heart is to Will One Thing*, (William Collins & Sons Co.) 1938, 27.

10. Ibid., 27.

22

Agape Love for God

THERE IS A SPECIAL kind of love for God which conducts us very quickly to the radiant center within ourselves in which God dwells. Some devotional writers have described this love as "incandescent," since it lights the way to God. It leads us into the Holy of Holies, the Temple of God where the *shekinah* (glory) radiates with undiminished brilliance.

We may describe this kind of love with the Biblical word *agape*, the essentials of which are that it is the love of God for us which expects nothing in return and is totally independent of any sense of worthiness or deserving on the part of the recipient. It is unconditional love, setting up no requirements which must be met in order for one to receive it. It is based totally in the nature of the giver and demands nothing of the recipient. It flows forth from the heart, in this case the heart of God, with an uninterrupted flow and has no reference to conduct or quality of our lives. "God so loved the world that He gave His only begotten son"[1] for the entire world despite its abysmal sinfulness in the grips of death, permeated by evil run rampant with no hope within itself of ever achieving even a modicum of worth or value. Yet "God so loved the world." His love flowed from his own nature without reference to the condition of its object. *Agape* depends totally on the subject and has nothing to do with the object.

How could we possibly love God then with *agape*? How could we ever love in such a manner? How could we mere mortals love with this kind of love so different from our ordinary understanding of love. In effect we must love Him with His own love since He is the author and only source of *agape*. Therefore we seek to love Him with "his great love wherewith he has loved us,"[2] that is, reflect back to Him the same love that He has extended to us. Like a mirror reflecting back the sunlight, we

1. John 3:16.
2. Ephesians 2:4b.

82

may cultivate the kind of reflectivity that returns God's own love to Him. In effect, this amounts to our allowing God to love Himself through us. We receive His love and redirect it upon Him and to Him. How can this be done?

We love Him in this manner by loving Him *as if* He were *useless* to us, as if He were of no help to us, as if we received nothing from Him. In short, we must bracket or suspend any sense of the blessings we have received or might receive from Him. Even the great blessing of redemption, the salvation of our souls, and all the marvelous occasions when He has delivered us, consoled us, upheld us, reassured us, and granted us peace, all these must be bracketed in an act of true *epoche*. Of course, we have gratitude and thankfulness for all His gracious mercies to us but we must act and think *as if* He were useless to us.

In doing this we love Him solely because He is God rather than the One from whom all blessings flow. If we love Him simply because it is a good deal for us to have Him on our side, then the quality of that love is really the quality of self-interest. If we love Him because of the good He does for us, then our "love" is self-serving, corrupted, and distorted and in fact may not be love at all. God, in that case, is our instrument, a convenient tool, a profitable asset, and we should not be surprised that this kind of "love" does not conduct us into the sacred sanctuary where we can meet Him in loving fellowship

Loving God as if He were useless to us brings us into the presence of the source of all the riches of glory which reside with Him in our hearts. Through this disinterested love, that is, love without usefulness, love without desire for rewards of blessing, we receive God and all the fullness of His grace and glory.

Classical devotional writers have referred to this instrumental kind of love for God with humorous but effective images. Meister Eckhart likens such utilitarian use of God to the use one makes of a cow:

> Some people want to see God with their eyes as they see a cow and to love him as they love their cow—they love their cow for the milk and cheese and profit it makes them. This is how it is with people who love God for the sake of outward wealth or inward comfort. They do not rightly love God when they love him for their own advantage. Indeed, I tell you the truth, any object you

have in mind, however good, will be a barrier between you and the inmost truth.[3]

Johannes Tauler put it this way:

> Know that if you seek something that is your own, you seek not God. You will never find Him. You are acting as though you made a candle of God to seek for something, and when you have found it, you throw away the candle.[4]

Making God into a cow or a candle, that is, using God as an instrument for achieving something else, however worthwhile it may be, falls far short of loving Him for Himself alone. Considering Him as if He were useless to us is an interesting technique to lead us to love Him unconditionally.

This love of God as if He were useless (shocking when put this way) produces *agape*. Since God can never be undeserving, unworthy, incapable of earning our love, or totally lacking in merit, we can never render *agape* to Him as He renders it to us. This is simply because *agape* is love that has no relevance to the worth of the recipient. God could never be like the unworthy sinner. Therefore, we must simulate that condition in Him. We do this by bracketing the blessing, benefits, and values He provides for us constantly. By temporarily disregarding this flow of blessings and good into our lives and viewing Him *as if* He were useless to us, we can love Him for Himself alone and not for His benefits. Then we are approximating *agape*, the kind of love He bestows on us. We love Him for who He is and not for what He gives. Considering that He is worthless to us, then we can bestow this Godlike love on Him, loving Him with the same love with which He has loved us.

Unconditional love opens an inward communion with Him which is radiant and vibrant. The radiance and vibrancy must, however, never be considered as an end in themselves, that is, they must never be sought for their own sake. They are the result of our unconditional love for God and not the object of our devotion or the desires of our heart. They are given as a result of our *agape* to God.

Remarkably, when we have given this absolute, single, and non-instrumental devotion to God, we discover arising within us a brightness,

---

3. Blakney, 241.

4. Cited in Kirby Page, *Abundant Living,* (New York: Farrar & Rinehart,1944), 152–53.

a vibrancy, a lilting melody of joy and peace. This experience has come almost simultaneously with the first instance of our rendering this affection to God as if He were useless to us. Having loved Him for Himself alone, our souls are flooded with all spiritual blessing. We are permitted to sit together with Christ in heavenly places, and in the heavenly place within our own hearts.

And how shall we describe more specifically this love to God which opens our awareness of His dwelling in us and our dwelling in Him? Our answer as to what it means to love God often seems vague and unconvincing. But thanks to Augustine, the great Christian interpreter, we have a very specific definition of what it means to love Him. Augustine asks himself "What do I love when I love my God?"[5] He answers:

> I do love a kind of light, melody, fragrance, food, embracement when I love my God; for He is the light, the melody, the fragrance, the food, the embracement of my inner self—there where is a brilliance that space cannot contain, a sound that time cannot carry away, a perfume that no breeze disperses, a taste undiminished by eating, a clinging together that satiety will not sunder. That is what I love when I love my God.[6]

Yet if we sought Him even for these admirable values, our love would fail. The light, the vibrancy, the melody, the fragrance, the embracement of the inner self, the breeze, and the satiety that does not come are blessings we diligently seek and rejoice in. But we must not love God because of them and in order to receive them.

The qualities of disinterested incandescent love traverses the inner distance and conducts us into the consciousness of the sacred presence. To rehearse them: a super-spatial brilliance coming from the *eternal elsewhere*, a music from cosmic spheres, a holy fragrance not dispersed by earthly breezes, a taste for the heavenly that is never satiated, an embrace by everlasting arms that does not tire us in its enfoldment of us. "That," Augustine says, "is what I love when I love my God." But if we loved God for *these*, we would be loving Him for His benefits and therefore loving ourselves.

Well did the anonymous medieval English writer say in *The Cloud of Unknowing* that, "by love may he be gotten and holden, but by thought

5. *The Confessions*, Bk X, Ch 6.
6. Ibid.

never."[7] Not only "by thought never," but also by willing, never; by demanding, never; by desiring, never; by works, never; by negotiation, never; or by anything else or everything else, never.

Only by the divine gift is the light, melody, fragrance, food, and embracement received. Enacted *agape*, the loving of God for Himself alone, the devotion to Him when all benefits and blessings are bracketed, that is, loving Him as if He were useless to us is what brings these things to us.

---

7. *The Cloud of Unknowing*, ch. 6.

23

Activating Spiritual Agencies and Powers

THAT THERE ARE SPIRITUAL powers, ministering spirits, heavenly agencies which are readily and instantly available to serve us in times of crisis is definitely referred to in the Bible. These powers, angels, *Logoi*, forces, all servants of God, which work on our behalf usually without our knowledge, are set in motion by God's grace and love for us. Just as the statement, ". . . while we were yet sinners, Christ died for us"[1] indicates that without our knowledge or consent, God acted graciously and redemptively on our behalf, so do ministering spirits, angels, agencies, and powers act on our behalf without our asking, and beyond our understanding. These are the secret actions of God in the blessing of His people. Just as this verse indicates: "The secret things belong to the Lord our God: but those things which are revealed belong to us and to our children forever . . . ,"[2] so the secret operations of God are the silent manifestations of His grace which operate to bring about our good.

In addition to these hidden operations of grace, we are given the privilege of calling on God to intervene for us in times of need. Indeed, this is one of the major objectives of prayer. We ask for help from God. We ask Him to employ the powers that do His bidding to help us in our times of extremity. And He does so. Sometimes His action is done secretly and we recognize it only sometime after the fact. At other times we become aware of His power being exerted for our benefit while it is occurring. Sometimes the "secret thing" continues to be God's secret and sometimes His actions are "those things which are revealed" and then belong to us.

1. Romans 5:8b.
2. Deuteronomy 29:29a.

Regardless of whether we are aware of them or not, divine powers operate in our individual situations just as they operate the universe and control reality as a whole in a larger context. But, of course, these powers are simply the instruments of God. They are not independent of Him nor do they constitute a hierarchy of beings who stand between us and God. We always have direct access to Him and these agencies and powers, angels and messengers are simply the avenues through which His gracious redeeming and delivering power is mediated to us.

An interesting instance of such divine intervention is reported at the conclusion of Jesus' experience of the Temptations. At the end of the ordeal when Jesus' strength was depleted and His spirit was weakened, the gospel writer records: "Then the devil leaveth him, and, behold, angels came and ministered to him."[3] On another occasion during His arrest in the Garden, Jesus referred to the possibility of angelic powers on which He could call to rescue Him: "Thinkest thou that I cannot now pray to my Father, and he shall presently give me more than twelve legions of angels?"[4] but He rejected this possibility for the sake of the fulfillment of the scripture: "But then how shall the scriptures be fulfilled, that thus it must be?"[5]

Jesus did not call in the twelve legions of angels because this would have disrupted the divine plan. But He did accept the ministry of angels after the Temptations. This episode becomes the paradigm for us when in times of stress and distress, we can activate heavenly powers to minister to us just as they did to Jesus. Having these powers of heaven working on our behalf, ministering to us, directing our path in life, arranging circumstances for our spiritual well-being is essential preparation for our entry into paradise with Christ. Acting in such a way as to activate them is an important step leading to our transcendent experience of being in paradise with Christ even while we continue our earthly life.

How then are we to engage these divine powers to minister to us? First, we should follow the example of Jesus set forth in His experience of being tempted. He repudiated every suggestion Satan made during this time of intense challenge. His resistance consisted of standing on the written scripture. Every suggestion from Satan was turned back with a direct, specific quotation from the Old Testament which was the scripture of

---

3. Matthew 4:11.

4. Matthew 26:53.

5. Ibid. 26:54.

Jesus' time. This reliance on the revealed Word of God (which He Himself had been the subject and source in His status as the Eternal Son) gave Him an unshakeable foundation on which to stand and He gave not an inch to Satan's attempts to induce Him to seek an easier way. The essence of the Temptations was to induce Jesus to find a short-cut to His ministry. It was an attempt to convince Him that the cross was not necessary and that He could accomplish His work in another way. But Jesus refused to compromise on His calling; rather ". . . he steadfastly set his face to go to Jerusalem"[6] and therefore toward the agonizing experience of crucifixion. Standing on the Word and being steadfast in our calling results in angels ministering to us, that is, divine powers and heavenly forces, spiritual agencies and entities working on our behalf. This is a valuable asset in the ordinary Christian life as well as an important step in being "taken up" in to heavenly glory, i.e., being with Christ in paradise. It will hasten the *today*, that is, the occasion of our transcendent experience, in making this day the today of eternal glory for us.

Secondly, when we are placed in an ultimate crisis situation and choose to preserve the soul rather than the body, then spiritual powers work both within us and outside us to support, undergird, and possibly deliver us from the threatening powers that have us in their thrall.

Living for the spirit, even to the extent that the physical body might have to be sacrificed, is an act of great magnitude. It opens spiritual doors to realities that we never dreamed existed. That is, it activates spiritual powers that operate both within our hearts and in the external environment that minister to us in very remarkable ways.

This principle can be succinctly stated in this way. If we choose the life of the soul over the life of the body, we activate divine powers that work both in us by strengthening the inner person and by making significant positive alterations in the outward circumstances we face.[7]

We have emphasized that this principle is operative in crisis situations when our very being is at stake and we know that this is a condition which makes the choice pointed and acute. Such a crisis situation provides the most dramatic instance of the principle's operation. However, it also works in other situations, such as the ordinary operation of our faith.

6. Luke 9:51b.

7. Mihajlo Mihajlov, "Mystical Experiences of the Labor Camps," *Kontinent 2,* (Garden City:Anchor Press/Doubleday, 1977). This article provides remarkable instances of the activation of divine powers in the stress of imprisonment in the Soviet Gulag.

These commonplace instances in the daily choices and commitments of our ongoing faith also activate God's acts on our behalf. In our constant choosing Christ over the lures of the world, in choosing the life of the soul over the life of the body, in choosing to follow the Lord rather than the way of the world, we experience the steadiness of this principle in operation. Daily ministry occurs within us and without. We are aware that heavenly presences and powers are at work in us and for us. But especially when these choices are intensified by threatening forces, then we experience in a much more convincing way the inner presence of Christ mounting up to fortify the soul and concurrently we see His hand rearranging the outer situation in which we find ourselves.

Internally, we find the "still, small voice"[8] becoming stronger and more clear. In ordinary times, this inner voice has become vague and distant as our own natural conscience has hindered and diluted it. It may have become nothing more than our own soul speaking to us. It may have been reduced to an inner dialogue with ourselves. It may be only our own conscience. But when we are put to the test, a test that involves our very existence, a test that calls into question our very being, then the still, small voice is no longer so still; no longer so small. It becomes the strong, certain voice of the divine, the voice of God, a word from beyond, an aggressive, assertive and absolute voice that is to be followed without reservation, without equivocation, without rational analysis, without "but what if," without the input of the intellect or common sense. We hear it and we follow it! And that is that! And when we follow it, then heavenly powers are showered abroad upon our life and circumstances. And then we know that ". . . He hath done all things well."[9]

There is no guarantee contained in this voice or the operations of the spiritual forces at work on our behalf that we will in fact be delivered from our suffering, trial or even annihilation. Such an outcome cannot be expected because God's operations on our behalf do not contain these assurances or promises. What is contained in this divine intervention is that whatever happens will be God's will for us and that it will redound ultimately to spiritual victory. Otherwise, why would He not have delivered the martyrs of old from the sword, the gallows or the stake? The life of the soul is the primary concern of God in all this. The body, the flesh,

---

8. First Kings 19:12.

9. Mark 7:37a.

the life in the world are all secondary and somewhat incidental in such a crisis situation where one's existence, one's very being must be affirmed and chosen.

In choosing the spiritual over the fleshly, the inner voice becomes forceful and authoritative, giving direction, assurance, empowerment, along with consolation and a deep sense of being in God's hands, as outward circumstances may be rearranged according to our needs. But it is all for God's glory, not our victory. And we must say with Jesus as he faced the Cross: ". . . not my will, but thine, be done."[10] And then rest in the everlasting arms of God.

After such an episode in Jesus' case, "Then the devil leaveth him, and, behold, angels came and ministered to him."[11] We can expect the same after we have stood fast, chosen the life of the soul over the life of the body, and followed the direction of the still, small voice which has become amplified and authoritative in the process.

10. Luke 22:42b.
11. Matthew 4:11.

24

Abandonment to God

THE SPIRITUAL METHODS AND practices we have spoken of previously were to be practiced in a piece-meal and fragmentary way, that is, a prayer here, a casting of a care on Him there, a remembering to turn within, a single act of praise, a resting on Him in a moment of crisis, a fleeting act of thanksgiving, and the like.

But now if we would prepare ourselves to be with Christ in paradise all these diverse exercises and activities can be comprehended in a single spiritual movement. We will endeavor to show how to commune with the eternal God within and cast all our cares on Him in a single act. No longer shall our spiritual practice be fragmentary and piece-meal, no longer here and there, "now and again, or "ever so often." But in a single act we can accomplish the entire enterprise, which we have previously described.

Even though we may have previously approximated abandonment of the self to God, we are now enabled by divine grace to achieve authentic and comprehensive surrender of our wills to His, our ways to His, our thoughts to His, our life to His.

We have a strong impetus to seek this blessed experience because of our desire to be "taken up;" to traverse the heavenly realm, and meet the Lord in intense personal encounter. We wish to abandon ourselves to God. Some spiritual writers have offered informative descriptions of their concept of abandonment and many of these may be helpful to us in the forming of our concept of just what we are attempting to activate in our own souls.

Madame Guyon, a seventeenth century French spiritual writer, offers a good treatment of abandonment of the soul to God, which she calls a "self-donation" and gives a provocative summary definition:

What is abandonment? It is forgetting your past; it is leaving the future in His hands; it is devoting the present fully and completely to your Lord. Abandonment is being satisfied with the present moment, no matter what that moment contains.[1]

To put it another way, abandonment to God is simply to have no other source of support but Him; to desire none other, to seek none other, to expect none other, to accept none other and to desire only what He desires and to will only what He wills.

The prolific American hymn writer, Fanny Crosby, expressed it well when she composed these lines:

Thou the spring of all my comfort,
More than life to me,
Whom have I on earth beside Thee?
Whom in heaven but Thee?[2]

Having no one on earth or in heaven but God and leaning solely on Him for both physical care and spiritual consolation is what being abandoned to God means. With all our affairs, great and small, turned over to Him, we now live in total confidence that from the moment of the act of total surrender to Him, He will become, not only Lord and Savior to us but also our daily manager, presiding over all events and affairs of our life. Everything we encounter in life from that moment onward is under His direction and rule. From that moment, we are able to rest in the assurance, in which the Apostle Paul affirms that, ". . . we know that all things work together for good to them that love God, to them who are called according to his purpose."[3] The term for "work" in the King James translation could be rendered as "being worked." Seen this way, the word boldly implies that things are deliberately being designed and shaped by the Lord for our well-being according to His purposes for us.

Abandonment to God is recognizing the fact that ". . . ye are not your own? For ye are bought with a price."[4] When we recognize this, then we actualize it in our self-understanding. Since we have been bought with

---

1. Jeanne Guyon, *Experiencing the Depths of Jesus Christ,* originally published as *Short and Very Easy Method of Prayer,* Gene Edwards, ed., (Golenta, CA: Christian Books, 1975), 35.

2. Fannty Crosby "Pass Me Not, O Gentle Savior," *The Baptist Hymnal,* 308.

3. Romans 8:28.

4. First Corinthians 6:19b–20a.

the blood of the cross, Christ's redemptive sacrifice, we are then under obligation to transfer title of ourselves to the new owner, to the one who has purchased us. We now act "under new ownership."

We now replace our plans and intentions with those God has for us. We surrender our wills, thoughts and acts to His control and seek to follow Him precisely in His steps rather than in our own. We endeavor as completely as we possibly can to turn ourselves over to Him and desire only what He desires for us.

The Biblical paradigm for abandonment to God is the experience of Jesus in the Garden of Gethsemane during his agonizing hours before the crucifixion. As He faced the cross, He momentarily seemed to be overwhelmed by the magnitude of the task set before Him. For an instant He considered some other possibility. Matthew's Gospel records the incident as follows: "And he went a little farther, and fell on his face, and prayed, saying, O my Father, if it be possible, let this cup pass from me! Nevertheless, not as I will, but as thou wilt."[5]

It is interesting that the word "nevertheless" is not high-lighted or emphasized. It is rendered in the "lower case," that is, there was no break in this sentence of Jesus' prayer. Before He finished the sentence asking the Father to consider the possibility of removing "this cup" from before Him, Jesus instantly knew that this could not be! So in the same sentence in which He asked for this consideration, He repudiated His own fleeting thought and reaffirmed that the will of the Father was supreme and paramount and must take precedence over His own human will which for an instant reflected a certain trepidation of the agony that surely was set before Him. He abandoned Himself to the Father. ". . . Not as I will, but as thou *wilt*."[6] This is the prototype and paradigm of our own abandonment to God. We are to surrender the content our own wills and embrace the content the will of God.

Some spiritual writers seem to think that if we suspend our own willing or choosing, then God implants His will in us. For instance, Meister Eckhart writes:

> . . . when he (one) has no will of his own, then God will command for him what God would command for himself. When I give my will up to the care of my prelate, and have no will of my own, God

5. Matthew 26:39.
6. Matthew 26:39b.

must will for me; so if he were to neglect me, he would be neglecting himself. So it is with everything; where I do not choose for myself, God chooses for me.[7]

This passivity is not exemplified by Jesus in the Garden of Gethsemane, who actively struggled to surrender His will to the Father's. That what God wills for me would be preferable than what I will for myself is a foregone conclusion but it does not establish the idea that my will is replaced by God's. Rather, I must constantly commit myself to deferring to God in an ongoing autonomous decision. I choose to do what God desires and reject what I desire. This is very different from removing a part of myself and installing the divine will in its place. It is also vastly different from a posture of passiveness. Jesus said in his prayer in the Garden—"not my will, but as thou *wilt*."

Choosing God's will in Jesus' thinking is not the replacement of *His* faculty of willing by that of His Father but the choosing of an action. Rather than thinking of the will as a faculty, a capacity, a psychic function, a part of the self, Jesus thinks of it in the Garden as an action to be undertaken. In Jesus' thought, He would *do* the will of the Father, not have a part of His being replaced by a part of the being of the Father.

In this sense God can will for us, and is happy to do so while we remain truly ourselves; truly human. Otherwise, God is doing His own will through us and we no longer have any responsibility for the action performed. Abandoning ourselves to God does not require that we give up a human faculty and have a divine one implanted. Rather it is that we bend our human wills to enact the desire, intentions and instructions of God. Abandonment to God then is the choice to conform to the wisdom of God in every respect and not a replacement of a faculty of the soul with a divine faculty.

This presupposes that we can know what God's will is and that we can know His specific intent and purpose for us as individuals. This requires that God communicate His intentions to us; that He reveal what He wants us to do. And of course we do have a revelation from God. He has given us His word which is contained in the Bible. There we learn of God's general and overarching will not only for us but for the entire human family and created order. He wills that we should come to know Him in salvation; that we should walk by faith and not by sight; that we should

7. Blakney, 3.

trust the Lord Jesus Christ as our Lord and Savior and welcome Him into our lives as a permanent and abiding resident in our souls; that we should celebrate the fact that He has made our hearts a temple of the Holy Spirit by his indwelling.[8] He is ". . . not willing that any should perish, but that all should come to repentance."[9] And that we should confess our sins in full assurance for the Bible says "If we confess our sins, he is faithful and just to forgive us our sins, and to cleanse us of all unrighteousness."[10] He desires that we should draw near to Him as He dwells within our hearts and that we should "cast all our cares on him" for He cares for us.[11] All the "great and precious promises"[12] belong to us and are communications of God's will for us. We can know this will of His and conform our own wills to His. We can disconnect our own desires and implant His desires into our willing process. It is our will, however, that does the action but we have adopted the objectives of the divine will as the objective of our will. We have made a daily practice of the injunction to "Trust in the Lord with all thine heart; and lean not to thine own understanding. In all thy ways acknowledge him, and he shall direct thy paths."[13]

In all this, it is *OUR* will that is conformed to His will. Otherwise, our humanness is compromised, that is, if God's will has been substituted for ours, then we cannot be said to be authentically human. We have become semi-divine. Our own freedom and responsibility is undercut and we would become perfect saints, doing only God's will, which would have now been substituted for our own. How could we be anything but perfect? This is not what full dedication and consecration of ourselves to God means. Rather, our wills must be made to conform to His will. This process is never total and complete. We continue to sin and "fall short of the Glory of God." But we are on the way to higher levels of sanctification as we daily practice the subordination of the objective of our will to the objective of His.

Doing God's will is an act of devotion, a consecration, a surrender to be accomplished in the grace of God. It is always *our* will doing *His*

---

8. First Corinthians 3:16.

9. Second Peter 3:9.

10. First John 1:9.

11. First Peter 5:7.

12. Second Peter 1:4.

13. Proverbs 3:5–6.

will. We remain human while acting according to the desires and revelations of our heavenly Father. We remain ourselves, but ourselves under the daily commission of God.

In his classic study, J. P. Caussade offers this observation which directly challenges the kind of self interest mentioned above:

> We must offer ourselves to God like a clean, smooth canvas and not worry about what God may choose to paint on it, for we have perfect trust in him, have abandoned ourselves to him, and are so busy doing our duty that we forget ourselves and our needs.[14]

It is a dangerous thing as far as our self-image and reputation in the community is concerned wholly to surrender ourselves to God, that is "to present ourselves to God like a clean, smooth canvas." We remember how Isaiah reported His word, "For my thoughts are not your thoughts, neither are your ways my ways, saith the Lord."[15] We may expand this to include "my ideals are not your ideals, my design for your life is not your design, my intentions for you are not your intention, my plan is not your plan, my purpose is not your purpose." Giving ourselves over to One who sees things totally different from the way we see them, who thinks with a different mind from ours, cannot be anything but a highly risky thing. To successfully abandon ourselves to Him involves ultimate trust and confidence in God and His purpose for us. Such daring seems foolish to the world, but we know that until we have achieve some degree of this radical surrender, we have not yet touched the hem of His garment.

---

14. J. P. De Caussade, S. J., *Abandonment to Divine Providence*, J. Ramiere, ed. (St. Louis: B. Herder Book Company, 1921), 82.

15. Isaiah 55:8.

25

The Bible, Preaching, and Holy Waiting

THE INDWELLING OF CHRIST within us is generally like a placid stream flowing gently and sweetly through our spirits, activating our life of faith. There is always the possibility, however, that this stream will overflow its banks and become a raging flood, a tidal wave of spirituality that propels us into the heights of the heavenly realm, leading us to stand face to face with Christ the Savior. This is the spiritual experience we have called being with Christ in paradise for which the soul was equipped in the moment of its creation when the life-giving breath of God was breathed into it, becoming its basis and ground and making the physical organism into a living soul. The several "spiritual practices" mentioned in the preceding chapters help prepare us for such an occasion but underlying these and all our desire for the transcendent life are the study of the Bible, the hearing of preaching and the attitude of holy waiting upon the initiative of the Lord.

The next several chapters consist of an attempt to offer a description of transcendental experience based on my own first hand encounter with the Divine presence, that is, of being with Christ in paradise.

Since I did not know that such possible blessings existed, I could not have made any conscious preparation for the stirring of God's presence within me. The classical mystics seem to have made deliberate preparation almost in the extreme, almost as if they could set a trap for God and as it were catch the Almighty in their disciplined spirits. I knew of no possibility. My religious tradition did not convey such information to me.

So no deliberate preparations, no exercises of discipline were made or practiced. I had no idea what to prepare for or what to aim at through spiritual discipline. My only asset in this regard was a fervent desire to know Christ better and to love Him more. Only God knew that His blessings to me would be among those things the Apostle Paul described as being beyond human seeing, hearing or conceiving: "But as it is written, Eye hath not seen, nor ear heard, neither have entered into the heart of man, the things which God hath prepared for them that love him."[1]

Since such glorious possibilities were beyond the comprehension of any human being, incapable of being known by any existing human capacity, they could not have been sought by me in any determined and specific way. Paul continued his explanation of how we see the unseeable, hear the inaudible and conceive the inconceivable: "But God hath revealed them unto us by his Spirit: for the Spirit searcheth all things, yea, the deep things of God."[2] This is what He did in my case.

God began to give me an attachment to the Bible, which grew increasingly intense until I could never find enough time to read it all I wanted to. During my lunch hour at work, I would go to my car on the parking lot and read it just as long as I could before going back to work. Also, He began to speak to my heart with emphatic force through the preaching of my pastor, Rev. Otto Sutton. Through Mr. Sutton's preaching, He drew me more and more firmly into the Body of Christ manifested in that local church congregation. He also gave me a quickened hunger for spiritual wholeness through a genuine and passionate longing in my heart for the Lord Jesus. Like Paul the Apostle, I was coming to be possessed by the desire, "That I might know him, and the power of his resurrection, and the fellowship of his sufferings, being made conformable unto his death."[3]

And a sense of "holy waiting" began to develop in me. This consisted of a sense of spiritual expectancy, which bore many of the marks of the "dark night of the soul"[4] as developed by St. John of the Cross. Of course, I knew nothing of this concept at that time and only could make this connection at a much later time. For me, this time was marked by a general loss of meaning (in everything except Christ and Him crucified). I seemed to be paralyzed in my mental life, my emotions seemed empty and disconnected from reality. My self-esteem was very low as was the general level of my affect. My condition resembled the state of nihilism expounded by the philosophers and as well as clinical depression.

1. First Corinthians 2:9.

2. Ibid. 2:10.

3. Philippians 3:10.

4. St. John of the Cross, *The Dark Night of the Soul*, passim, trans & ed. E. Allison Peers (Garden City, NY: Image Books, 1959).

But this state of mind was somehow overridden and undergirded by the expectation that something more was about to occur. Intuitively I knew that my present state could not continue and I had a reassuring sense that something more was soon to present itself to me.

I continued to go through the motions of my job and the routine of life. I felt an intense loyalty to the church services and was reluctant to miss any service, even for good reason. I continued to be devoted to a simplistic and naïve reading of the Bible and held to a completely literal and surface interpretation of the scripture, and, of course, I eagerly anticipated every sermon of Rev. Sutton. All these practices were undergirded by the lively expectancy that an immanent spiritual event of great importance was just on the horizon.

Of course, I might have been contented with my job, the love of my church, the Bible, and the hearing of preaching. But these two aspects of my situation would not permit me to feel at ease—the longing in my heart for a more intense fellowship with Christ along with greater knowledge and commitment to Him and a *holy waiting* which anticipated some fulfillment, the content of which was yet undisclosed to me. These required a further fulfillment. They carried a promise of more to come, but I did not know what or when.

After several months of increasing love for the Bible, commitment to the church, deepening response to the preaching of the gospel, and heightening of the longing in my heart to know Jesus Christ more completely, along with a clearer comprehension of the interval of holy waiting, the Lord moved very dramatically in my heart. I had returned home from my night class at the University Extension Center. It was around 10:00 o'clock but still I read a passage of scripture, silently prayed and studied a section of *Systematic Theology*[5] by A.H. Strong. Then I went to bed, expecting nothing more than to rest for I was working hard on my job and attending night school. I was very tired. I dozed off to sleep, but to my great surprise was awakened by very strange but wonderful occurrences that shook my soul to its very deeps and set my life in an entirely new direction.

---

5. Augustus Hopkins Strong, *Systematic Theology*, (Philadelphia: The Judson Press, 1907).

26

Slapped by an Angel

A T THE FIRST STIRRING of the Eternal within us, we know that something quite extraordinary is going to happen and, indeed, is already
in progress. We know intuitively, almost before anything has occurred
that we are going to be made ". . . to sit together in heavenly places in
Christ Jesus."[1] And in quiet ecstasy we wait for the unfolding of the seamless garment of the experience of the Eternal.

Sometimes this first stirring is preceded by a quite unexpected
shock—a startling of our being somewhat like being slapped suddenly
on the head. This is the first stage, and instantly one feels the presence of
God with shocking clarity. Immediately we are brought to the recognition
of a sparkling vitality, a shimmering but powerful aliveness we have never
experienced before.

On the very first occasion of God's special revelation of His presence
in me, I did feel this sensation of being hit firmly and forcefully on the
head. This was so very pronounced that I arose quickly from the pillow
with a momentary sense of anger demanding to know who had done that
to me! Before I could express my demand, however, I was instantly aware
of a new feeling within me; a kind of "tingling warmth" in the area of my
physical heart. Instantly I recognized a new presence, not with me, but
rather within me.

The sense of being struck on the head was very distinct. Sometime
later I remembered the verse in Acts, which lead me to believe that a
similar experience had occurred to the Apostle Peter: "And, behold, the
angel of the Lord came upon him, and a light shined in the prison: and he

1. Ephesians 2:6b.

smote Peter on the side, and raised him up, saying, Arise up quickly. And his chains fell off from his hands."[2]

After this first episode, I realized that everything for me had been changed. I had an overwhelming convictional certainty that I had been called to the ministry which I had been contemplating. I knew that I would have to get a college education and beyond but there was no possibility of full-time study for me. I had been attending night classes at the University of Tennessee evening school held at the medical school in Memphis. I decided to join the Air Force in order to get the G.I. Bill benefits.

In a matter of days, I was at Lackland AFB in Texas and in a few months was sent to England. I began to preach in local Methodist and Congregational churches in the area and continued for the three years I was in England. My regular Air Force Specialty Code was Chaplain Services Specialist, roughly equivalent to church secretary in civilian life. Aspects of various intensity of my original experience continued to be given to me and were a source of great reassurance and joy.

Just before the end of my overseas tour in England, I was sent by the Air Force to Cambridge University to attend a week-long course entitled "Great Powers in World Affairs." This was not only a great series of lectures by very prominant professors (held at Madingly Hall, Cambridge), but it was the richest week spiritually since my original experience. While I had been very frequently blessed with repetitions of the original experience throughout my military service, this week at Cambridge was the capstone of my time in England. I would soon be returning to the United States to begin my college and seminary work so it was a special time of preparation. Madingly Hall was a retreat-like setting in an great mansion outside the town of Cambridge. Away from the noise and distractions of the barracks, the setting was ideal. Throughout the week, I was drawn over and over again into the paradise of the quiet and deep spiritual ecstasy; not emotional exuberance, but a deep and solemnly joyful sense of being in the divine presence and having the presence of the Divine in me. When I returned from Cambridge, my orders to return to the US and be discharged were waiting for me.

While I was on my way home from England where I had been stationed for three years at RAF Station Sculthorpe in Norfolk County, I was waiting at the base near Manchester for my flight home. There was to be

2. Acts 12:7.

a lay-over for the night. At the Base Exchange, I bought a copy of William James' *The Varieties of Religious Experience*.[3] Since I had not been to college or seminary, I was not familiar with this great classic. I spent that evening avidly reading it. One can imagine my great surprise and sense of excitement when I discovered that James had found that many of the people he interviewed for his research had reported just this same aspect of the experience, i.e., of being struck on the head at the beginning!

These two discoveries, one from Acts and one from William James, were valuable as supporting data long after my initial experience. I had more or less assumed that I was the only person in the world who had had such an experience. It was a comfort to know that others had had similar encounters and this gave me a stronger sense of the validity of what had been happening in me. Happily, the experience occurred very frequently while I was in the Air Force, usually without the sense of being struck (this may have been a feature reserved for the original occasion). But each time, the sense of total newness and the feeling of being gloriously blessed overwhelmed me.

At the first occurrence in Memphis, I had no criterion by which to interpret it. I knew only that from that first moment of being struck that the Lord was doing something in me and consequently with me. I knew also that this was the most glorious thing I would ever experience in this earthly life. I rejoiced that I was most richly blessed, according to some standard of selection that I could not know, to be chosen as the theatre for this great divine drama of visitation by the Lord, God of the Universe, Father of our Lord Jesus Christ.

No sources have been used in describing this spiritual experience. I have endeavored to report exactly and only what occurred in me and to me. Therefore, the singular "I" could have been used throughout. However, since I am now sure that many others have had similar experience, I decided to use the plural "we" in presenting the main aspects of the episode. The singular "I" is used to present my own preliminary states of mind and situations as well as actions taken in response. But when I say "we" I mean myself and any others who may have had similar experiences of being "with Christ in paradise," composing "a great cloud of witnesses."

3. William James, *The Varieties of Religious Experience*, (New York: The Modern Library, 1936).

27

Light from the Deeps Below Being

W E BECOME AWARE OF the warm presence in our heart which sparkles and tingles and this in itself would constitute a fantastic blessing of a visitation of the Eternal. As we enjoy this strange warming of our heart, doxologies begin to flow out of our consciousness in automatic, spontaneous praise of the One who has honored us with His presence. Thinking that this is an end in itself, we are not just satisfied but ebullient at containing the Holy Spirit. But then we are shaken out of our satisfaction by a diminutive spark of light arising somewhere paradoxically both within us and at the same time beyond us in infinite deeps. This curious occurrence also has unusual aspects: it both fascinates, draws and attracts us and produces awe and a kind of terror, similar to the state of soul described as *mysterium tremendum et fascinans,*[1] loosely paraphrased by me as the mystery which repels us by its overwhelming character and yet at the same time draws us to itself.

However, we are not disturbed by this, but remain calm and serene to an extraordinary degree. We know it is God making Himself known and we are not frightened—just entranced. This luminous pinpoint continues to shine with an increasing brilliance like Jesus' garments at the Transfiguration which sparkled with a shining ". . . so as no fuller on earth can white them."[2] We are no longer a spectator to this pinpoint of light. We watch it with complete fascination. It is contained in depths beyond our comprehension, so far away from us but at the same time so near. We watch it in its sparkling splendor for an incalculable amount of time. It sparkles and shines, radiating warmth and joy, and we are transfixed

---

1. Rudolf Otto, *The Idea of the Holy,* John W. Harvey, trans. (New York: Oxford University Press, 1958), 12–40.

2. Mark 9:3.

by its splendor and depths that seem infinite. Yet at the same time, we perceive it as underlying our being.

We intuitively perceive that these are the eternal deeps that underlie the soul and form its foundation and ground. We are totally captivated by its beauty and profundity. After some unknown amount of time, very suddenly, and it very gently it breaks through the lower limits of our being and enters from the vast depths below. Now it is clearly within us, but at depths we had never begun to imagine. It is clearly both within us and beyond us—beyond us not in terms of heights but in depth. It is clearly below our being, yet contained within us.

The luminous pinpoint sparkles silently and effortlessly in the vast measureless depth of the soul. And its curious double character is clearly apprehended and intuitively understood, that is, it is within us and yet beyond our being. It has "come" from the infinity below and now penetrates our fragile existence for indeed "we have this treasure in earthen vessels," entering our being from the deeps below.

It is clearly a spiritual light and as soon as it is recognized, it begins to increase in intensity. As it does so, it seems to come with steady ascent toward our being and, then, in an effortless surge, it crosses the threshold and enters our being from below. No longer do we comprehend it as in these deeps below being. It is now very clearly with in us, but we know it comes from unfathomable depths below us, which depths are nevertheless still ours.

Of course this luminous pinpoint is laden with divine power and attributes, causing the soul to sing, to praise, to consecrate, to bow down, to rejoice, to celebrate. Great hymns of the church such as "All Hail the Power of Jesus Name,"[3] along with a simple chorus affirming "No Never Alone, No Never Alone, He promised Never to Leave Me, Never to Leave Me Alone" ran through my being persistently. One might have supposed the Hallelujah Chorus or some other exalted, majestic angelic chorus would have been heard. But no, just a simple Training Union chorus and ordinary hymns. But holiness, majesty, divinity of God, grace, glory, and otherness were everywhere to be apprehended.

It was quietly and effortlessly done, directly and without the usual human emotions. The experience brings a totally new set of *ad hoc* feelings, emotions, and responses: quiet acceptance, joyful receptivity, and

---

3. Edward Perronet & John Rippon, "All Hail the Power of Jesus' Name," *The Baptist Hymnal*, 200–2.

objective observation. It is almost as if one were watching and observing, rather than participating, in the divine drama occurring within. We are *there* but it is a different kind of *thereness*. It is a special kind of presence, the essence of which was to *watch* as God works His work in us.

We are not afraid, but feel more serenity, more acceptance, and more grace than we ever could have imagined. The Holy Spirit has quietly remained in the heart, powerfully irradiant and full sparkling vitality. His presence causes the heart to overflow with quite inner praise to the Lord God. The luminous pinpoint, having entered our being from below, is proceeding so to speak *upward*, drawing ever closer toward the heart where the Holy Spirit is revealing Himself in glorious arrays of light.

As the luminous pinpoint continues His ascent, the brilliance of His presence continues to increase beyond human comprehension. He is a light not so much seen as felt. It is a vision not apprehended with the eyes, but with wholly new spiritual faculties we did not know we had. We cannot know if we have had these faculties from the beginning or if they are newly given in and with the experience itself. The divine visitation apparently provides the requisite special faculties required for its apprehension, the natural faculties being insufficient. Neither the natural eye nor ear nor heart can comprehend what God has done.[4] So, spiritual faculties are supplied by the Spirit, either in the original creative act or in the moment before us. Godly capacities which allow us to participate in this divine drama are provided by God.

Now we begin to perceive this light as ontological; as the *Logos* of creation. In the ascent of the *Logos*/light we vaguely thought of ourselves as Jacob's ladder. Not that we are climbing Jacob's ladder as the song announces. Rather, we are the ladder, and the *Logos*/light is climbing *us*. Our being provides the rungs of the ladder on which pre-existent *Logos*, God's eternal Word, moves upward toward the heart where Jesus Christ the Lord, triumphant in redemption through His cross and resurrection, is waiting by means of the Holy Spirit's mediation. The creator moves incessantly toward the redeemer where they will be joined in the Divine Reunion. Such interpretative images came later, after subsequent reflection, but in the actual experience one is only aware of the amazing ecstasy which is being "spun off" or emanated as the process is occurring.

4. First Corinthians 2:9.

During this part of the episode, the Holy Spirit has continued His warming and loving presence, marking time as it were, while the luminous pinpoint, the *Logos*/light has continued His ascent, coming closer and closer to the heart. It soon becomes evident that the light intends to join Christ and the Holy Spirit in the heart. But at this moment, the *Logos*/light, now much stronger than the original luminous pinpoint, has not yet entered. Although in relentless advance, steadily ascending, He remains in the precinct of being *below* the heart.

The *Logos*/light begins to seem personal. He has been within the depths below our being since our creation, just as He has been with every living soul. But now in this experience He has come into our being itself and He is still advancing through those depths we could not have known to exist. Although we are fantastically stirred and exhilarated in these overwhelming moments, we are somehow aware that He is going further! He is advancing toward the center of the soul, the sacred room of the heart. All the while the ecstasy is becoming more intense.

Rising ever higher with a relentlessness that could not be resisted, He is generating a quiet inner ecstasy. The mind is in a placid disengagement. We are in total passivity. The total self is wholly open to the Divine Visitor.

Sin has been confessed at the beginning of this episode. The soul feels itself cleansed and forgiven. All sense of guilt and regret are gone. We remember the words of John in his epistle: "But if we walk in the light, as he is in the light, we have fellowship one with another, and the blood of Jesus Christ his Son cleanseth us from all sin."[5] So there is no operative and unforgiven sin to hinder the ecstasy God desires to share with us.

We feel that we are actually present at creation, more specifically our own creation. We are Adam! We are the clay figure in the book of Genesis! We are the mannequin into which God breathed the breath of His life when I, and all human beings became living souls! The drama of the breath/*ruach* of God is reenacted in us. Later, when the Light (now seen as person) enters the sacred room, we will experience all over again being crucified with Christ! We will experience all over again being buried with him. We will recapitulate His resurrection.

But for now this experience is both intensely spiritual and ontological, that is, it has to do with our existence and the foundations of humanness, which are being stirred, shaken and rearranged.

5. First John 1:7.

We are permitted to rest for a moment as the Light from below hesitates for an unknown period of time. While He hesitates, the entire being celebrates what has occurred so far with silent, inner songs of praise and affirmations of adulation for the One who has entered the depths from below and has produced revolution within us. The soul pleads that this ecstasy might continue forever. We are truly exhilarated at having a reenactment of the first pristine moment of our existence and to experience own our birth as human with such sparkling clarity. We are lifted up into heavenly and eternal realms that we could never have imagined before these occurrences.

Occasionally, in an objective moment the mind registers a thought— a sense of wonder, but generally it is caught up in the celebration to such an extent that it is quiet in happy surrender and eager receptivity.

The body seems strangely alive. One would have thought it would have been virtually abandoned. Instead, muscles are alive with steady power. The senses are vital and dynamic, responding to every aspect of the situation. After an initial pounding of the heart, it now seems to purr quietly like a well-designed machine. The emotions swell with praise. In no sense do we lose identity of body or soul. We are more ourselves than we have ever been before. The Lord does not absorb us into Himself or reduce our selfhood to nothingness.

The Holy Spirit is marking time as He waits. While He does so, He is stirring up more joy and praise within us than we ever supposed ourselves capable of experiencing. Our praise is automatic and silent, not exuberant or vocal. But we believe that the pre-existing ontological *Logos*/Light is about to unite Himself with Jesus Christ the Redeemer, now the triumphant Lord dwelling in our heart through faith mediated by the Holy Spirit's presence.

The distinct and definite feeling is reemphasized that this divine drama is not happening to us but rather in us. We think of ourselves as a theatre for the divine self-experience, an arena in which God's experience of Himself takes place with a complexity we cannot describe. For a moment we ponder the notion that all spiritual experience is the self-experience of God, that is, the unification of the persons of the Godhead within the being of an individual in whom the experience occurs.

The original sense of being mere spectators of the divine self-experience was a fleeting impression, since our feelings were instantly so vitally engaged. We were overwhelmed by appreciation at being chosen as the locale, as the theatre for God's experience of Himself within our soul. The common music of familiar hymns and songs continue to fill our awareness and but soon are amplified with the power of grand symphonies of heavenly harmonies, ringing with the power of the music of the spheres. We are being transfigured in the process. The Lord, the eternal Word, the *Logos* of God, the Creator is moving upward within us. The creator God as Father, Son and Holy Spirit is moving toward the Redeemer God as Father, Son and Holy Spirit for a Divine Reunion at some yet unrevealed heights.

28

The Ontological Light Enters the Heart

WHILE EVER ADVANCING AND steadily ascending, the *Logos*/Light is still below the heart. He is still in the ontological depths—the dimension where our being as human, where our living soul is generated. He remains the creative breath of God now made alive to our awareness. At this level, the divine presence transports us into the very act of creation itself, now enacted in our own souls. We are truly present at our own creation. What we are feeling is eternity itself. Since the edges of time have been removed, we are in fact in eternity. We are being taken into the throne room of the Eternal.

But now! Now, some startling new thing occurs! The *Logos*/Light moves higher. He enters the lower reaches of the heart itself. Even while the ontological depths are still warm and glowing, stirred with the movement and motion of the creative word that gave it existence and being, the divine presence now moves into the heart. This action seems to have a spatial dimension. He has moved from the lower depths of being to a higher level, that is, into the area of the heart.

And this is interesting to note: A change seems to come over the divine presence as this "distance" is traversed. No longer is He only the ontological source of our being, now, as He enters the heart He becomes Redeemer, Savior, Lord, King of Glory, Christ of the Cross, Resurrected Jesus! No longer only the Source of Being, but now Friend, Companion, Indwelling Hope of Glory! As in the previous episode, we think of ourselves as present at our own creation, as a participant and witness to our own coming into being as human, as an observer of our own beginning, as recipients of the divine inbreathing. Now, however, we experience ourselves as being made new creations in Christ as we recapitulate that pristine moment in which we first believed. We are present at our own crucifixion, having died with Christ in the act of being born again. Our faith commitment is reenacted. We are present also at our own resurrection, having been risen with Christ. We feel the immediacy of being "raised to walk in the newness of life."[1]

"Holy, holy, holy, is the Lord of hosts: the whole earth is full of his glory,"[2] we proclaim with the cherubim and seraphim. There is no terror, no forbidding awe, no blinding holiness. Rather, love, light, and unsurpassed joy are the elements of our experience.

Brilliance and ecstasy, the brightest light and the purest joy are united and expressed in this luminous pinpoint. But now, after having penetrated and obliterated the lower boundaries of our being, this luminous presence is now flooding the whole soul. It is no longer containable, no longer localized, but now totally pervasive, drenching the total self with joy, light, and power. Every nook and cranny of the soul is filled and our total organism is quietly but fully alive with doxology and praise to God.

Having broken into the heart itself, the presence from below moves upward with forceful deliberateness. Like a slow but invincible wave, it pulsates with power as it overwhelms the heart. After having crossed the boundary between the ageless, endless deeps below us, Christ has risen into our being, totally captivating it.

Probing everywhere, searching out dark recesses and hidden dimensions of the soul/heart, He tries and tests every aspect of our life and thought. He opens the closed, exposes the secret, and enters the forbidden. Searching the heart, He is filling every nook and cranny with this divine light and heavenly warmth. Like "liquid love"[3] being poured out within us, like fluid light running through the conduits of the soul, like tropical sunshine the warmth of His person radiates and sparkles! And it is all happening in us!

What can we do but sing and rejoice? Again the heart rings with automatic praises. The mind soars with extravagant affirmations of the wonders of divine grace! The body is taut with more life than it has ever experienced before. We are overwhelmingly real. We are not a spirit or a spectre! We are physical organism containing an inbreathed living soul. The source of this soul is playing upon His creation as a lyre, strumming

1. Romans 6:4b.

2. Isaiah 6:3.

3. Charles G. Finney, *The Memoirs of Rev. Charles G. Finney,* (New York: A. S. Barnes & Co., 1896).

us as if we were a golden harp! The author of our salvation is ratcheting up His accomplishment in us to new levels—to unheard of heights!

After an indeterminate time, we rest for a moment to consolidate the gains of this and the previous episode in the deeps below. The *Logos*/light from below has begun to fuse with the triumphant redeemer. And, of course the *Logos*/light and the redeemer are one and the same divine being, each bearing the fullness of the Godhead—Father, Son and Holy Spirit. We were not aware of any distinction of persons of the Trinity and every episode was performed by the fullness of the Divine. In His omniscient understanding, God knows we need a brief respite from the rigors He has produced to our entire existence, to our total mechanism, by this visitation. So He gives me a moment of rest. We return to a comfortable plateau, receding from the peaks. Light/joy quietly radiates through us totally. We are embraced by the oceanic vastness of what has happened to us. We are calm, collected, and radiant with an internal harmony of all the elements of our existence.

Then an unexpected thing happens! A whole new episode apparently is about to begin! We had thought the experience was finished when He had reached the heart. But no! Now a new ascent begins. We had been concerned from the time He entered the heart as to whether our soul could endure the experience.

Could our chest contain the thing being accomplished in us? Would our hearts burst in the process? It was a genuine, if only momentary, concern. When we considered it in an instant's reflection, we realized that if in fact the experience resulted in our death, we would only step forward into the full glory of which we were now receiving only a partial expression. Partial, not because of the holding back of the divine presence but because of the limited capacity of the vessel into which the experience was being poured.

Apparently, a part of the probing and searching previously mentioned was a testing of the capacity of the heart to receive such an experience. In His grace, God would not kill us with His presence. The scripture makes several references to God's protective limiting and hiding of Himself in order to preserve the one He approaches. He demonstrated what He already knew, that is, that we could survive His embrace. But it had been an early concern later dispelled by the remembrance that if in fact, one died in the act, a higher glory than was possible while we inhabit the earthly tabernacle awaited us beyond the last breath.

The new thing was a higher ascent than we had experienced this far. It was an ascent higher than the movement in the ontological deeps below being, higher than the wonderful warming and filling of the heart. Where would He go now? What dimensions would He traverse, taking us with Him?

I later gave a name to this dimension. I later called this "the heights above the heart." At the time of its beginning, however, I did not think of a name for what was about to occur, nor could I have done so because I did not know what was about to happen. Even though the mind was fully itself with the addition of a singing and celebrating sense of exhilaration and spiritual, otherworldly happiness, only an eager receptivity and now a newly activated fascination with what might happen next occupied the thoughts.

As the ascent to the heights above the heart began, again the concern arose concerning my survival. Could my chest cavity, indeed my body as a whole, contain and withstand the tremendous expansiveness that the *Logos*/Light produced. Later, I realized that this was only an apparent effect on the body, paralleling and instantiating what was occurring in the spirit/soul/mind. But again I thought, "surely my heart will burst!" "surely my chest will explode!" But then the comfort of knowing that if those events should occur, that occurrence would be embraced and contained in the actions of God and He knew quite well what He intended to accomplish in me.

29

To the Heights Above the Heart

T HE BRIGHTEST LIGHT AND the purest joy are united and expressed in this luminous pinpoint. But now, after having penetrated the lower boundaries of our being, then entering the heart itself, this luminous presence is flooding the entire soul. No longer containable, no longer localized, it now pervades the entirety of our being, drenching the total soul/self with supernal light, power, and joy. Every nook and cranny of our existence is filled with the Divine while our total organism overflows with doxology and praise to the God who is now within us. God is within us with an overwhelming fullness and to an extent that we could not have conceived with our own faculties.

We could not have imagined this occurrence with our merely human faculties. The eye could not possibly see it; the ear could not possibly hear it; the intellect could not possibly comprehend it. Only the event itself could have communicated our knowledge of it. Suddenly a new thing occurs! The steady glowing brilliance has quietly illumined the heart with light/joy, begins to move in a clearly discernable pulsation.

The light/joy seems intent on withdrawing from its highest point. However, the divine departure is only apparent, but it is pronounced enough to elicit a felt alarm as to its possibility. Instantly, we thought to blurt out like Jacob, who at the Brook of Jabbok, holding on to the Divine Wrestler exclaimed, "I will not let thee go, except thou bless me."[1]

Lacking the self-assurance of Jacob and his aggressiveness in relation to the Eternal God, we cannot command a blessing, as he seemed to do, but only reach out in loving but unspoken pleas for the visitation to continue. These pleas were not verbal but rather the reaching out of the

---

1. Genesis 32:26b.

heart as if to prevent His escape from our being, as if to keep God there where He had always been, though never before with this intensity.

Now He begins to make preparations to go beyond the heart. Before He does so, however, He builds a firm foundation in the heart from which He will journey to heavenly regions far beyond us. And He will take us with Him! (We know this only in retrospect because this is in fact what He did).

As He begins to make preparations to go beyond the heart, we are concerned again that our heart may fail under the expansive pressure of this intense light/joy. Again, the chest seems incapable of containing such a reality. There is concern that the heart may burst. In the next moment however we again lose all concern for life. We desire only to experience whatever else there is to come. No longer concerned for life, we gladly resolve to receive all that God wills to give us.

The holy presence, the full Godhead—Father, Son, and Holy Spirit—continues to probe, surging over the heart with giant but gentle swells like breakers on the ocean shore. He fills every dimension of the heart, moving us to tears with warm and touching power. He is completely irresistible now. But we have not wanted to resist Him at any point. Rather we feel carried along with Him as He traverses the various stages and dimensions of our being. From the very moment of being "slapped by an angel" any slightest reticence to enter the exalted realms of the holy and heavenly was overcome by a fascination fueled by the desire to experience the ecstasy that remained.

As the divine presence throbs in the heart, there is a new aliveness everywhere. The powers of the physical body seem heightened. The mind rushes with silent affirmations of praise and is quick in its operations. The emotions are quiet and steady with rejoicing in glad songs of surrender and consecration. Gratitude radiates through the soul, which marvels at having been chosen to experience in our own spiritual faculties this superb journey of God to God. Wonder, gladness and awe mingled with humility at being chosen to be the theatre for this divine drama fill our consciousness. Occasionally words of prayer form in our consciousness, but such words are rare and generally reflect that which we are feeling with "sensations" too deep for words. These feelings are different in kind from the ordinary feelings and sensations. They are beyond the power to verbalize. Words are secondary. This experience cannot be verbalized and words seem to be something of an intrusion into the domain of holy feeling.

The prayers occurring now are primarily prayers which are felt; prayers given by the one to whom the prayers are directed. God dictates our prayers to us and we understand the passage in Acts about the Holy Spirit interceding for us with groaning too deep for words.

All fear subsides. The strength of the Eternal is granted in precious promises intimated to us without words. Light/joy are joined by all these other eternal resources and are blended into a splendid symphony as the harmonies of the eternal realm ring through whatever being and existence we have, expanding it and consecrating it. For some considerable but indeterminate time the glory is maintained as He thoroughly saturates the total being with spiritual power and grace. Over and over He assaults the supposed limits of the soul.

Then, after the highest peak has been scaled and His purposes are completed, the divine climber begins a descent. The recessional begins as light/joy begins to fade, producing feelings of both relief and sorrow. It is a relief that the intensity of the presence has lessened with the realization that our hearts are not going to burst after all. And sorrow at the thought that the episode may be ending.

But the journey is not yet finished! We are delighted as the surge of light/joy begins to advance again. An altogether more powerful upward thrust is felt. This time it explores new spiritual space within us. It reaches a much higher level than at its previous high. The heart sings again, the mind is strangely calm, and the body is alive with a vitality previously unknown.

After reaching this new high, the light/joy recedes slightly, but only momentarily. Then it thrusts upward once again, reaching a higher level on each subsequent movement.

Several times the process is repeated. Each time the heart is overwhelmed more dramatically than the previous one. The chest seems quite capable of bursting at the apex of each upward thrust, but the next even higher stage is easily accommodated as the divine visitor provides the capacity to receive Him.

Over and over again, we suppose that the upward surging has reached its highest possible level. We believe that it can proceed no higher. We imagine that the final apex has been reached. But we find that we are mistaken. The rising Lord proposes to go further. We remember the disciples on the Emmaus Road, as Jesus drew near. Luke reports that ". . . he made as though he would have gone further."[2] And here within our own being, "he made as though he would have gone further." And further and higher He goes.

Finally in the greatest of all these surges, the heart is totally surpassed. Light/joy goes beyond the heart itself. Beyond the heart, yet still somehow within us, the Lord advances, entering the heavenly place. He takes us with Him. We know that we are being transported to heavenly realms above and beyond, yet this realm above and beyond is still within us. At its climax, we are both in the body and out of it. We are both on earth and in heaven. We are both in time and eternity. We are both in God and have God in us. We are both alive and dead.

We are empty of ourselves, yet perfectly full. We are void of all desire, all self-assertion, all self-interest, yet full of the divine; full of God. Filled to the brim and much beyond, our soul has overflowed into Heaven. We sit together with Christ in heavenly places. In Christ we are in Heaven. In Christ, we behold the glorious! We are filled with it! We overflow with His glory! Our seemingly small souls have been opened upwardly and we traverse the golden shore.

We have no idea how long we dwell in these heights above the heart.

Regardless of how long in time our presence there continued, it was long enough. It was a timeless moment—an eternal interlude. And we wished we could continue there forever! But the final recessional begins.

Not all at once does He go. Without a doubt, He knew that such an abrupt withdrawal would destroy us. Having experienced such fullness, we could not bear instant emptiness. And He is not ready to receive us into the divine realm as a permanent resident. So He begins a gradual withdrawal; an incremental recessional.

As He had surged by degrees in the ascent, so does He withdraw by degrees of recessional. The waves of light/joy continue to pulsate with slow, certain rhythms. But with each wave, the highest level is slightly lower than the previous one. Over and over again the process continues until at last we feel Him leave from below. But we also know that He doesn't leave at all, for "Christ in you, (is) the hope of glory."[3]

He returns to the ontological deeps—the deeps below being, to empower and operate the soul as its basis and ground where He has dwelled

2. Luke 24:28b.

3. Colossians 1:27b.

since the first moment of our existence. At the same time, He returns to His abiding dwelling place in the heart, which He entered in the day of our salvation to carry on communion and friendship with us. And, of course, He returns to the holy place in eternity, which He has never left.

Rather than departing, however, we soon discover that He is in fact intending to remain with us forever, dwelling in the heart with greater clarity, vivacity, and power than we could have ever imagined. And we are so glad, and so greatly blessed for we know that we shall never again be the same as we were when this episode began.

Everything now is forever different. We have been called to new dimensions of redeemed existence. And we are with Him eternally, for He is with us forever. We are deeply convinced that we have been called to an unimaginable newness of life, to unwavering consecration, to discipleship and sacrificial service unto death. We are so glad!

From the ontological deeps below being, to the immediacy of the heart, and now to the heights above the heart, the Godhead has traversed our being. He has made His journey through us and has taken us with Him into the heavenly places and we shall be with Him forever. In the meantime, there is life to be lived. There is work to be done. Let us be up and doing! For Jesus Christ is with us!

Again we think of Jacob, who, after his remarkable dream of the ladder reaching up to the sky, remarked, "Surely the Lord is in this place; and I knew it not."[4] In our case however, we knew it was the Lord the instant he began to stir in the ontological depths.

As for us, for me, my mind is left calm and chaste. My heart is warm and yielded. My emotions are relaxed with a sense of well-being and blessedness. My body seems highly tuned yet relaxed with a warm feeling of perfect adjustment and unusual harmony. I feel very good indeed in every way. I have the firm conviction that Christ will never leave me and that I have been with Him in the eternal realm, and that sometime in the future I will be with Him there forever.

". . . Even so, come, Lord Jesus."[5]

4. Genesis 28:16b.
5. Revelation 22:20b.

30

The Light Divine

". . . God is light, and in him is no darkness at all."[1]

I KNEW VERY LITTLE of mysticism. I had since high school read mostly the Bible and Sunday School literature, but I did have a growing desire to know Christ better and as I have said elsewhere, an intense devotion to my church and the preaching of my pastor. This was nothing unusual for my time and place. But then, suddenly, into my heart the Lord came bursting. I readily knew who He was. He was the Light, the Holy Light, the Divine Light the scripture had spoken about. I later described Him as the Light/joy. I knew intuitively it was God—Father, Son, and Holy Spirit—which had come upon me very quietly after an original bombastic entry into my being. I had made no deliberate preparation. There were no exercises; no deliberate mortification of the self.

In the sincere longing for Jesus, everything necessary was contained and activated. He honored that and came to me. Except for a superficial understanding of a few Biblical passages, I had a very meager concept of the Divine Light. I did very little interpretation of it except to note that God appeared as light, without image, form, pictures, bodily shape, or any human features. He was light. This did not bother me as I understood that He was invisible to the physical eye. This is why I did not *see* God. I was feeling Him, experiencing Him, embracing Him, deriving unimaginable joy from Him, but I did not *see* Him. Later reading of mystical theology confirmed that God manifested Himself *only* in the form of Light. This is the only element of His being that we could experience and then I re-

---

1. First John 1:5b.

membered the Biblical witness to the light. ". . . God is light, and in him is no darkness at all.[2] This quotation is true to the Biblical revelation:

> In so far as God reveals Himself, communicates Himself and is able to be known, He is Light. It is not by analogy with physical light that God is called Light. The divine light is not an allegorical or abstract thing; it is given in mystical experience.[3]

Such statements as this, which ring true to my experience, were of great help to me in the subsequent interpretation of what happened in those episodes.

We know from scripture that we cannot see Him with our physical eyes; not with these organs in our heads. We can, however, *feel* Him as Light, apprehending Him and being apprehended by Him, utilizing totally different faculties, that is, the eyes of the soul, the inward spiritual eye. Yet we do not *see* Him at all. We feel Him as Light, but not with the usual senses. Just as the word of God creates its own context in which to occur, and the Spirit of God composes its own community, so the Divine Light produces its own environment and furnishes the faculties required for its apprehension. Human faculties cannot receive or contain the Divine Light. Neither can they cause it to appear. Religious devotion or spiritual exercises cannot bring Him forth into the soul, nor can the most fervent desire and longing bring Him to us. His appearing as Light is always a generous gift of grace, at a time and place of His own choosing. God maintains His complete sovereignty with respect to His appearing as in every other aspect of His dealings with the world.

In my early descriptions of my mystical experience, I began to use the term *Logos*/light and Light/joy. I understood that my visitor was the eternal *Logos* of God, the creative power, which formed the world and the soul. I perceived that His presence did not just *communicate* joy to my soul, but rather, that the Light *contained* joy as an inherent and inseparable feature. And my soul was flooded with joy as the Divine Light made His procession upward through my being, entering the heart and surging in undulating thrusts upward to eternal regions beyond my heart, all the while taking me with Him.

---

2. First John 1:5b.
3. Lossky, 220.

Some classical writers on mystical experience suggest that without love the Divine Light is not real and genuine.[4] To me, love is *contained* in the Light. The same is the case with truth, power and all the other highest features of faith. All the divine endowments are inherent in the Light, inseparable from it and communicated in and with it. Some writers also suggest that the Light can be turned away from and rejected.[5] My experience confirms to me that no one would ever resist this in-pouring of grace and glory even if they could resist it. This Divine Light consumes the supposed freedom of our wills. At the same time, we are never more free, than when we willingly surrender and open ourselves to His gracious approach. We throw everything to the wind when God offers Himself to us and invites us to become His earthly habitation and at the same time begins taking us upward into the ecstasy of paradise.

As naïve as I was in the beginning, I had come to know some Biblical passages that refer to the Divine Light. For instance: "In him was life; and the life was the light of men,"[6] and "That was the true Light, which lighteth every man that cometh into the world."[7] Also, "The Lord is my light and my salvation . . ."[8] And, "For God, who commanded the light to shine out of darkness, hath shined in our hearts, to give the light of the knowledge of the glory of God in the face of Jesus Christ."[9] So there was a growing awareness of the nature of the Divine Light. I understood it as both the ontological basis of the human soul (derived from John 1:4 and 9) as well as the indwelling presence in our hearts based on faith which results from our acceptance of Jesus Christ as Lord and Savior.

A favorite passage of mine was and is this: "But is now made manifest by the appearing of our Saviour Jesus Christ, who hath abolished death, and hath brought life and immortality to light through the gospel."[10] Since He is the light, He brings all things into the light. Without the light of Jesus Christ, everything appears distorted. But he brings everything into the light so that it may be correctly seen. He has brought immortality

---

4. Theologia Germanica XLI, CCEL/t/theo _ger/theolo47.htm.

5. John Tauler. *The Inner Way* XI, CCEL/t/tauler/inner_wa/inner-18.htm.

6. John 1:4.

7. Ibid., 1:9.

8. Psalm 1:27a.

9. Second Corinthians 4:6.

10. Second Timothy 1:10.

to light, demonstrating that man should live forever but that when he fell into sin, he fell under the bondage of death. When Jesus died on the cross, He abolished death and thereby brought immortality to light. It was illuminated and made plain.

Also many of the hymns we sang in church refer to this Divine Light. Hymn writers made frequent references to the Divine Light. "Holy Spirit, Truth Divine; Shine upon this Heart of Mine," "Send the Light," and "The Light of the World is Jesus" are good examples.

Naturally, I found Augustine's theory of illumination unsatisfactory since it does not accord with the Biblical view. For him, the human mind had no difficulty in knowing physical objects but with eternal truths such as logic and mathematics, the mind was incapable of knowing these in its unassisted state. Hence, the Divine Light was provided to the mind by God. He illumined the mind so that it could know unchanging realities and eternal truths.

Such Light contains no knowledge of itself. We have it, according to Augustine, but we don't know the Light itself. It is at the beck and call of everyone. It is engaged whenever anyone considers an eternal truth such as $2 + 2 = 4$. We are not aware of its operation and therefore can't know its source or origin in God. This is not what the Bible means by Divine Light.

According to my experience however, the Divine Light is not an epistemological function. Although we read ". . . in thy light shall we see light,"[11] this has to do with the issues of reality and redemption and is not primarily a reference to intellectual knowledge. It is not primarily related to knowledge. It is about the state of the soul. It concerns the entire spirituality of the person, not just the process of knowing the rather specific eternal truths.

It is about being called, commissioned and sent. " Lord, send me," is the most appropriate response. The Divine Light is about the spreading of the gospel. Its objective is evangelism, the proclamation of salvation, and service to God. It is therefore a call to serve the Divine rather than a process for knowing specific truths of a certain kind. In Augustine's theory of illumination, every human mind has this capacity to engage the Light without reference to faith in Christ. It is a dimension of the mind as such and therefore unrecognized and unacknowledged by the average person as a divine gift. This is not the same reality the Biblical concept of the Divine Light points to.

11. Psalm 36:9b.

Usually the Divine Light is experienced internally, but sometimes it is external. For instance, Moses' face was shining when he came down from Mount Sinai with the tablets of stone. "When Moses came down from Mount Sinai, with the two tablets of the testimony in his hand as he came down from the mountain, Moses did not know that the skin of his face shone because he had been talking with God."[12] Later the Apostle Paul refers to this, explaining that the veil was to hide the fading glory of the Divine Light in Moses' face.[13]

A more contemporary occasion of which I am aware of and was peripherally involved in, is a an interesting example. Although I was retired from the pastorate, I held a funeral for a member of my former church. The deceased man's wife was hospitalized at the time and could not attend her husband's services. The funeral home made a videotape of his funeral. A few months later when the family decided to watch it, they reported that the Spirit was palpable during the playing of the video. Everyone was deeply moved and later when the family retired for the night, the wife began to glow with a strange light. Her face, upper body and even her hair sparkled with a light like which those in attendance had never seen. They immediately and intuitively interpreted this as a manifestation of the Divine Light, the very manifestation of God's presence in that difficult situation. Several months later the wife also died. This incident was reported to me at the interment service at the cemetery by her sister-in-law who was with her at the time. Although I would have liked to have heard more about it, it was difficult to get details with many other people milling around. Nevertheless, I took great comfort in being a part of this manifestation of the Divine Light by conducting the original funeral, which apparently was used by the Lord as a vehicle for His appearing. Everybody there that evening when it occurred was moved and deeply touched, as I was on hearing of it.

Also, as reported and described in a later chapter, I have experienced over the years of my preaching ministry the continuing sensation of a warm glowing feeling on my lips. I was never aware that there was a visible manifestation accompanying this but my heart was always warmed and touched simultaneously. I took this as an approval of my preaching and sometimes as an encouragement or, perhaps more often, a challenge to do a better job of proclamation of the gospel.

---

12. Exodus 34: 29 RSV.

13. Second Corinthians 3:13.

31

Amazed in the Presence

"**G**REAT IS THE LORD and greatly to be praised in the city of our God, in the mountain of his holiness."[1] How sweetly was your grace given to me, O Lord, that made the city where I was your city for me, and the slightest hill the mountain of your holiness! Great you are, indeed! And greatly are you to be praised. But how could I praise you? With what resources could I exalt your holy name and sing of your surpassing glory? Now I know the answer! Since it is your holy and eternal right to be praised, you praised yourself through me! You, yourself, O Lord, were the author of the praises which flowed so wondrously through the corroded circuits of my life! Even though I was scarcely more than a by-stander in the process, nevertheless, I became a beneficiary of your boundless grace!

What did I, who received immeasurable gifts of the stirring of your self in me, have to offer you, the Eternal One? Only this—a broken self, consisting of numerous conflicting fragments, lacking a well-formed center, existing very precariously! Always in immanent danger of serious disintegration; always on the edge of the precipice, ". . . without were fightings, within were fears,"[2] I recognize that often I had only a very tenuous, an extremely fragile, connection with reality. Among the many selves I seemed to be, none was strong enough to step forward and affirm, "I am you!"

Having nothing positive I could offer you, O Lord, I could offer you only negations; only my needs—great gaping personal needs! Little did I realize that this is exactly what you wanted from me—just my needs. But I

---

1. Psalm 48:1.
2. Second Corinthians 7:5.

erroneously supposed that I must bring something of value to you so that I might be worthy of your blessings.

Somehow, despite my blindness, you lead me to bring to you the only thing I could—simply my broken and needy self.

Since I was in no position to expect anything from you, O Lord, I certainly did not expect the outpouring of your presence, the very stirring of the Eternal, of you, yourself in me during that beautiful autumn season in the place where I lived—Memphis, Tennessee.

Most fortunately, O Lord, your grace had already been given to me and was steadily at work to make me more whole emotionally. You had already made me fully whole spiritually, granting me full pardon for my sins and giving me complete acceptance with you through the Lord Jesus Christ. But I had not yet been able to accept my acceptance. But I had not yet fully apprehended the one who had apprehended me.[3]

But I had this one resource—I had heard the gospel of your son, the Lord Jesus Christ and had believed in it with childlike simplicity, for indeed, I was a child at that time. I had died with Him on His cross and have risen with Him in His resurrection as your servant Paul so aptly describes in Romans. [4] Through repentance and faith I had most surely received the unsearchable riches of Christ! Genuine conviction of my sins, more or less agonizing, certainly very disturbing had begun to arise in my heart at the age of twelve. Now, with unswerving certainty, I knew that Christ had born by griefs and carried my sorrows[5] on the cross, setting me free from the bondage of sin and death and in the process giving me the life eternal.

Although I was poor in personal endowments, you had made me very rich through Him who had Himself been rich but became poor for my sake.[6] Through all these years, you must have been leading me to tell of your excellent greatness revealed in my own experience. You know that I have tried before to describe your working within me—for my own private devotion—and how our human language has failed to express the inexpressible!

---

3. Philippians 3:12.

4. Romans 6:1–11.

5. Isaiah 53:4.

6. Second Corinthians 8:9.

Was not my acting on your grace sufficient? Did I have to explain it too? You know that when you came to me I instantly happily surrendered to you, becoming your virtual prisoner, in joy and celebration at having been chosen. In a matter of months (9 to be specific) I found myself in England facing monumental challenges with great opportunities to preach as I was convinced that you had called me to do. And I had preached only two sermons before this! But your great people on the Hunstanton and Docking Circuit of the Methodist Church graciously received me and gave me great encouragement, although of course my efforts were halting and very inadequate, even embarrassing, certainly to me and probably to you and to Jesus! But was not this obedient response to your call enough? Was it not sufficient to act on this experience, even to the extent of totally changing and remaking my entire life? You must have expected me to write about it, to describe what you did in me, to share my deeply private inner life with others.

But it was not totally a sinful reticence, not totally blinded eyes, not totally a selfish treating this as a private resource for my own edification alone. It was not totally a distorted and unbecoming spiritual modesty that kept me from telling of your excellent greatness to me, O Lord. No, it was more specifically the inadequacy of our language to convey what you had done in me. And of course added to that was my own lack of facility in the usage of that language.

Also, as I began to learn a little psychology in school, I realized that many would say, based on psychological research that could be cited, that all this was merely a subjective episode with no divine dimension— merely the struggling of a deprived soul to find some foundations in re- ality—merely a psyche seeking identity and defense mechanisms, seeking permanence in the midst of turmoil and confusion. "Nothing happened" they might say. "It can all be explained in terms of abnormal psychology," they might affirm. Rational arguments seem inadequate against such claims of immanent subjective processes. But I have found nothing in the writings of Freud or Jung, or Neitzsche or any psychologist or philoso- pher that can defeat my conviction that you were working your divine purpose and flooding your grace, love, light, and power in me then and in many subsequent occasions.

But I hesitated to advertise this most intimate and private encounter with you and that because I supposed you wished for me to keep it to myself. Some may have used similar occasions for pride and spiritual arrogance and that I wished to avoid.

Later, when I became a pastor, I would occasionally refer to my spiritual experience. But I noticed how strangely my congregation would respond to any reference to this private encounter with you. Any mention of such experience seemed to make them nervous and coolly distant. During my pastoral years, people seemed to want only affirmations of familiar orthodoxies and any reference to your special visitation seemed to cut across their understanding of the Christian life. Once, when I asked a member of my church to read a manuscript of mine which referred to my special experience with you, she was baffled as to why I had not preached about this. I do not remember my answer but perhaps it had to do with the notion that my experience was not the subject matter of preaching. So I kept it to myself as my own private treasure from the Lord. I did not share this with the members of my churches but it was the spiritual resource from which I was constantly drawing.

Now, O Lord, you seem to have enabled me to put into words, however inadequate, that which has been in my heart for these many years. Our secret will be no longer ours! This experience is so deeply private! And in fact beyond words! Beyond telling! But you seem to want it told. You seem to want it told to others. As my own years wind down and all the experience of life on earth dies with us, I leave this record and report. It was on your initiative that you came to me and now I understand that it is on your initiative that you are prompting me to tell the story!

Perhaps some good may come of it. But that is in your hands, O Lord, not mine.

My prayer is that you will glorify yourself through this presentation and that your son Jesus Christ will be praised because of it. Amen.

32

Answering the Call

AFTER SUCH AN OVERWHELMING experience of being taken up into the divine glory, one must return to the ordinary everyday world with some sense of being chosen for some specific mission. Apparently the return to the common life is accompanied by this sense of a holy calling. It was not necessary for me to deliberate on the meaning of what had happened to me. I did not need to contemplate the response which would be appropriate. The sense of calling came in and with the experience. Indeed while this original episode was occurring, rejoicing raced through my consciousness over having been chosen.

For some, such as myself, this could be nothing less than the calling to the Christian ministry I had been previously contemplating. I could interpret my being "taken up" into the heavens as nothing more or less than a confirmation that God had called me to be a preacher. So like multitudes of others, I immediately began to respond to this sense of call.

I was twenty-three years old and had no college work except the few courses in accounting and business administration in the night school at the University of Tennessee Center at Memphis. After my experience, I felt the need to quickly begin Biblical study at the college level. I learned that Union University, a Baptist school, was offering Bible classes in Memphis. After investigating, I discovered the location of these courses and called about them only to discover that the enrollment period had just ended and therefore I would have to wait until the next semester to begin. This was very disappointing to me because I had a sense of urgency. I felt the need to act immediately. But these events, as it turned out, proved to be an instance of a window being closed, only to have a surprising door open.

But the wholly unexpected door which opened had an unusual feature—the entering of it was not optional. It was a door that had to be entered. Within days, I received my draft notice for the military. I was classified 1-A, that is, available for immediate induction into the Army. This development struck me, not as a hindrance to my sense of call, but rather, a divinely guided step in its activation. After consideration of any options I had (and the only one I had was choosing which branch of service I would enter), I decided to volunteer for the Air Force and joined immediately and left Memphis on very short notice for basic training at Lackland Air Force Base in Texas. Throughout the course of these twelve weeks, I felt sure that I was there because the Lord had put me there, although I was sometimes baffled by the seeming irrelevance of the program to what I imagined the fulfillment of my call would be. Although I was of slight physical build, I was able to hold my own throughout this entire episode and seemed to gain the respect of my fellow trainees.

At the completion of basic training, I applied for the vocational field of Chaplain Services Specialist and was chosen to be trained that area. After a brief assignment to Biggs Air Force Base, El Paso, Texas, (which seemed like a dead end to me at the time) I received orders to go to England which I welcomed with a sense that something significant was about to happen. I was assigned to RAF Station Sculthorpe in Norfolk County, England, where I found many churches without pastors whose services were conducted by lay preachers. I discovered that the Methodist church in the area had only two ordained ministers serving twenty-five or more small churches, most of which were served by local lay preachers who were assigned on a rotating basis through a Quarterly "Plan." On discovering that I was a candidate for the ministry, a Methodist chapel at the village of Syderstone asked me to preach after which I signed up to be a "local preacher" on the Hunstanton and Docking Circuit of the Methodist Church on which I preached once or twice almost every Sunday for the three years I was at Sculthorpe along with occasional appointments interspersed in local the Congregational church at South Creake as well. Reverend John Wynn was the Superintendent of the Circuit and was of great help to me. I kept my preaching in the churches very quiet at the Base Chapel where I was assigned because I did not know how the Chaplains would react to it. One Sunday, the Base Chaplain, Major Dwayne H. Mengel preached at a church where I had preached and they naturally mentioned that I had been there. On Monday, Chaplain Mengel, whom I admired greatly and whose example was a strong influence on me said, "You have been hiding your light under a bushel" and commended me on my efforts. I had a sense of real though tentative activation of my call during that time. (Twenty years later

I returned to Norfolk County, England for a preaching tour of the churches where I had preached while stationed there). Also, I taught an adult Sunday School class on the Base in the Chapel program and I worked full time at the Chapel as a Chaplain's Assistant, my regular Air Force job. I considered these as a valid response to my spiritual experience and was very happy to be doing the work at hand although I was somewhat frustrated by the delay to my theological education.

I did, however, acquire two years of college work through the University of Maryland at the Education Center on the Base and received the "Maryland Medallion" for academic achievement. We were fortunate to have American instructors who were in England on sabbatical leave or for research. But many courses were taught by professors from nearby Cambridge University. Near the end of my tour, I was chosen by the Air Force to attend a short course at Cambridge University entitled "Great Powers in World Affairs." Living at Madingly Hall with a private room in an academic setting was conducive time for revisitation of the Divine Presence. The time at Cambridge was rich with spiritual elevation and occasions as powerful as my original encounter with the Holy occurred again and again. Once more, I considered that the purpose of this intense period was to prepare me for the changes that were at hand. After returning to my Base, my orders were ready for me to return to the US and be discharged from the Air Force. I left England with a certain sense of melancholy because the three years had been so rich and satisfying. Twenty years later I would return to preach at many of the churches on the Hunstanton and Docking Circuit, and also at the Base Chapel at Sculthorpe.

As my Air Force group was waiting to board a flight from Manchester to McGuire Air Force Base, New Jersey, we had several hours of layover at Manchester. I happened to see a book at the Base Exchange (I might have heard the title somewhere but since I had not been to college full-time or finished a degree, I did not know of this work). It was William James' famous *The Varieties of Religious Experience*. I bought a paperback copy and read it breathlessly during the layover and on the plane. It seemed like a miraculous confirmation of my experience and gave me unbelievable joy. What an inspiration it was! I was not familiar with mystical literature at the time and felt alone in my experience. I might have thought I was the only person who had had such an experience, but now I came to understand that there was an entire community of such persons as myself. This gave me many assurances and I was moved very deeply by James' research. None of the reported experiences were identical to mine, but there were many similarities and it made a lot of difference to me. I could go on to the rest of my calling with a deepened certainty concerning its originating experience and validity.

This was four years after the initial episode. We landed at McGuire on July 4, 1958 and after a few days at home, I was assigned to Blytheville AFB in Arkansas for processing out of the military. After spending the remainder of the summer at home with my parents, I entered Baylor University. Returning to full-time academic status was a great strain and stress to say the least. It was difficult to manage six courses of study. The first semester, I took Old Testament, New Testament, Greek, Logic, Ethics and Religion 137a (a practical course in ministry). I graduated in two years and then went to Southern Baptist theological Seminary and finished the three year degree there. These seminary years were among the richest of my entire life and I found frequent occurrence of my spiritual experience refreshing and affirming.

My first church was Talbot Park Baptist Church in Norfolk, Virginia, where I served three years as Associate Pastor and then went on to be Pastor of other Baptist churches. I earned additional degrees at the University of Missouri (MA and Ph. D residence) and Union Theological Seminary, Richmond, Virginia (Doctor of Ministry). After twenty years in the pastorate, I taught philosophy and later world religions and Biblical studies at a community college for twelve years and in other colleges as a sometime Adjunct Professor. Since retirement, I have held several interim pastorates and presently teach a Bible class in my local church and am attempting to write.

Of course the direction and focus of my life was totally changed by my experience. And I feel sure that everyone else who has had such an experience has fulfilled some sense of calling, some to vocational Christian service, some to humanitarian endeavors, some to medicine, missionary service, various helping professions, but always "living the difference," of being a kind of marked person, although none would have flaunted their blessing and most would have kept total silence about it, because it is so intimate and personal and also because it is very nearly impossible to capture the essence of what happened to us in words. I have said all this simply to indicate that the primary response, I, and no doubt others, who have had such an experience is to understand that experience as communicating some holy calling. (It never occurred to me that there could be any other reason or purpose for it, although I now realize this was a rather impoverished understanding of spiritual experience).

My spiritual experience did not make me a saint nor endow with any additional talents, abilities or capacities, except perhaps the capacity to bear up under difficult circumstances and to pursue my vision without serious deviation from the course. The work was hard and required grit and determination. The sense of call carried me through many difficulties and helped overcome many obstacles.

Of course, in addition to outward response to the call, there were spiritual changes within me which consisted of a continuation and possibly a heightening of the faith I was already actively practicing. My faith was naïve and simplistic but very real and sincere. I really believed that the Lord calls us to special services and was waiting expectantly for such a call. Perhaps some might think of my mystical encounter with God as simply wish fulfillment or a kind of self-fulfilling prophecy. I could only say that the character and intensity of my feeling of being in the presence of the Divine was such that surely it is beyond the capacity of the unaided ego to achieve. It was something "wholly other" as far as I knew and I have found nothing in literature or experience to make me change my mind. And the fact that my experience was not just a one-time event but consisted of recurring episodes over many years, I think, adds additional confirmation of its validity.

33

Coals from the Heavenly Altar

A FTER HAVING BEEN CAUGHT up into the presence of the Eternal, we must return to the light of common day. We might have desired to remain forever on the mountain top, but now we must return to the valley. We may have expected to be allowed to continue forever in the presence of the divine splendor. Our souls eagerly grasped God and would have fervently held on to Him without ever returning to the troublesome world of which we are still a part.

In His wisdom, however, God brings to an end the marvelous episodes of the visitation with Him in His own domain of the heavenly. Apparently God does not will for us to stay with Him in the heights of ecstasy forever. He does not want us there continually. In addition, our souls could not endure undiminished glory. We would soon be destroyed by the splendor of His presence in the brilliant intensity of the highest moments of our experience. So He sends us back to earth. I considered each subsequent occurrence of my experience to be a confirmation of my calling, an empowerment of my ministry or a further calling to some specific task.

Although the embrace of the Divine occurred on many occasions in the early years, with more or less regularity, the full envelopment of my being in the divine glory occurred less frequently after my years in the Air Force. As a young man in a distant land, preaching in churches, which were substantially different from those I was used to, I needed divine support and reassurance. But as is reported by leading mystics, so it happened with me, that is, there were fewer instances of this ecstatic visitation in due time. But it seemed to me that after I returned to the United States and entered college full-time and then went on to seminary, I needed the continued embracement of God. But apparently God does not want us to become dependent on such high moments. So, although the experience has occurred intermittently until this present day, it did so with less frequency.

A new aspect eventually developed and has continued to into the present. On crucial occasions especially in those situations related directly to my calling, I have felt a touching of my lips with a feeling of light and warmth, a sensation which is quite strong and certain. I have never doubted that it is a spiritual touching which I have interpreted as either an affirmation of my preaching ministry or a challenge to greater commitment.

This experience of the warm touch of my lips has been the continuing reflection of my full experience of the overwhelming presence of God. After the first several instances of this experience, I remembered a Biblical text that suggests a precedent. In Isaiah, we read: "Then flew one of the seraphims unto me, having a live coal in his hand, which he had taken with the tongs from off the altar: And he laid it upon my mouth, and said, Lo, this hath touched thy lips; and thine iniquity is taken away, and thy sin purged."[1] While Isaiah's experience produced a cleansing from sin, I did not have the sense that that was the purpose of mine. Rather, it seemed to be an empowerment for the mission, which I had undertaken in response to my call. But the structure of the two occasions is similar and I have considered Isaiah's a prototype of my own experience of the burning lips which is accompanied by a gentle but pronounced sensation of light and warmth in my heart. But this burning of the lips is greatly reduced from the full soul experience described in preceding chapters. I am sure the soul could not receive this overwhelming experience repeatedly without being burned out and ultimately destroyed. So the different version is desirable and celebrated.

The warmed heart is a common occurrence among Christians of course and has precedents in the experience of the disciples on the Road to Emmaus when they said, "Did not our heart burn within us, while he talked with us by the way, and while he opened to us the scriptures?"[2] We read of John Wesley's "Aldersgate experience" after which he reported, "My heart was strangely warmed."[3] This was a crucial turning point for Wesley, but multitudes of ordinary Christian believers can report this

---

1. Isaiah 6:6–7.

2. Luke 24:32.

3. *John and Charles Wesley*, 107.

same experience of the strangely warmed heart. In multitudes of churches throughout the world, whenever and wherever Christ is truly preached the warmed heart occurs. It is the common treasure of the entire church. But I am not aware of anyone reporting the burning of the lips, but I am sure that this must have occurred wherever Christ's yoke is accepted and His calling is heard and responded to.

34

Night in Gethsemane

CHRISTIAN BELIEVERS ARE SUBJECT to the same ailments, both physical and psychological, as all other mortal human beings. Depression, emotional disturbances, and despondency are possible states of mind for everyone. The dark night may descend upon us despite our faith. The cold winds of mental distress may blow across our consciousness and temporarily disable and displace the warmth of God's love and grace, overriding previous exalted spiritual experience and plunging us into the darkness of alienation and aloneness during which we must walk a lonesome valley, resembling the valley of the shadow of death.

Even after having achieved a considerable spiritual advancement, we may fall into a surprisingly thick darkness. This state of soul can occur at any stage in our upward journey from the most rudimentary steps to the highest level with Union with God. The higher we have reached, the deeper we may descend.

Soon after the exhilarating experience of conversion with all of its ecstasy which may accompany entrance into the life of faith (so comprehensive and radical as to be called "passing from death unto life" or "being born again"), we may find ourselves walking among the shadows of the valley. The mountain top on which we stood just a short time ago is now only a memory (but a special kind of memory, i.e., a memory with a promise of recurrence). We have the assurances of the indwelling Christ who assures us that He will be with us always: ". . . for he hath said, I will never leave thee, nor forsake thee."[1] Therefore we are preserved in the time of dryness as we wait in full assurance that we shall once again receive the showers of blessing, the light of Christ and the victory.

---

1. Hebrews 13:5b.

Ordinary Christian believers find this alternation of the mountain top and the valley of the shadow occurring in their spiritual experience. But the mature ones rest in the assurances of Christ even when those assurances seem vague and far away. Devout believers are able to move forward on yesterday's faith, to hold out during periods of aridity on the basis of the spiritual rains that they have previously enjoyed. Even when faith seems to have lost its vitality, the memory of better days sustains true believers. Knowledge of past experience of God's gracious support, remembrance of brighter days sustain them and enable them to confess like the Apostle Paul that "I know whom I have believed, and am persuaded that he is able to keep that which I have committed unto him against that day."[2] Cognitive awareness of the extent to which grace has revolutionized our life and being gives us the blessed assurance that Christ is sustaining us even when we cannot recognize or experience it operationally at any given moment.

These episodes however never reach the intensity described by St. John of the Cross in his famous treatise entitled *The Dark Night of the Soul* as follows:

> The darkness, which the soul here describes relates, as we have said, to the desires and faculties, sensual, interior and spiritual, for all these are darkened in this night as to their natural light, so that, being purged in this respect, they may be illumined with respect to the supernatural. For the spiritual and sensual desires are put to sleep and mortified, so that they can experience nothing, either Divine or human; the affections of the soul are oppressed and constrained, so that they can neither move nor find support in anything; the imagination is bound and can make no useful reflection; the memory is gone; the understanding is in darkness, unable to understand anything; and hence the will likewise is arid and constrained and all the faculties are void and useless; and in addition to all this a thick and heavy cloud is upon the soul, keeping it in affliction, and, as it were, far away from God.[3]

In the modern world this might be diagnosed as clinical depression, a psychiatric illness, and appropriate treatment would be undertaken. St. John of the Cross, however, considers this to be a spiritual step on the

---

2. Second Timothy 1:12b.

3. St. John of the Cross, *Dark Night of the Soul*, ch XVI, trans. & ed. E. Allison Peers, 3rd Rev. Ed., (Garden City, N.Y.: Image Books, 1959).

way to the ultimate spiritual goal of Union with God. During this time of spiritual darkness, the soul is gathering powers, which will lead it to the pinnacle of its journey beyond time and space to the very gate of heaven where it will be embraced in a face-to-face encounter with the Living God and thus be united with Him.

In considering the Biblical material, we find that there is never an occasion in which the soul's faculties are totally overwhelmed by any state of mind the person is enduring. There is always a basis for hope, the apprehension of an open door and a lively expectation of deliverance soon to come. This sense of deliverance is what distinguishes Biblical examples of suffering from that described by St. John of the Cross.

What prevents our dark night from being an ultimate collapse of the soul's functions is the expectation of deliverance or at least the interest of the Divine in our situation to whom we appeal, even though His aid may be delayed. Yet it is the expectation of God's ultimate intervention on our behalf that instills hopefulness into the dense darkness of our present situation. Jesus prayed on the Cross, "My God, my God, why hast thou forsaken me?" His acknowledge of "my God" expresses Jesus' knowledge that His loving and caring Father maintained a continuing interest in the event which had befallen Him (as well as the Father's own participation in it to the ultimate extent). Although Jesus was experiencing an absolute sense of being abandoned and alienated from the realities in which He had previously trusted, His plea to "my God" attests to a living faith that there would be a victorious conclusion to the situation in which He now found Himself.

Likewise when the Psalmist wrote, "Why art thou cast down, O my soul? And why art thou disquieted in me?"[4] No doubt his mind was benumbed by his depression; his will partially paralyzed or at least deeply hindered in its ability to act and choose; his emotions were detached, distorted and artificial in tone. But in the remainder of his sentence he expresses confidence in a solution to his dilemma as he instructs his soul to ". . . hope thou in God: for I shall yet praise him for the help of his countenance."[5]

4. Psalm 42:5a.
5. Ibid. 42:5b.

In the famous Twenty-third Psalm the writer acknowledges that, although he is walking through the valley of the shadow of death, he has divine accompaniment and protection.

And the Apostle Paul described his situation in vivid terms:

> We are troubled on every side, yet not distressed; we are perplexed, but not in despair; Persecuted, but not forsaken; cast down, but not destroyed; Always bearing about in the body the dying of the Lord Jesus, that the life also of Jesus might be made manifest in our body.[6]

Yet he was assured that God would make it right.

> For which cause we faint not; but though our outward man perish, yet the inward man is renewed day by day. For our light affliction, which is but for a moment, worketh for us a far more exceeding and eternal weight of glory; While we look not at the things which are seen, but for the things which are not seen: for the things which are seen are temporal; but the things which are not seen are eternal.[7]

Christians are able to claim, assert, and rejoice in divine comfort even in their moments of darkest despair, alienation, and aloneness. This is what distinguished modern Christian experience from the medieval experience described by St. John of the Cross as one of ultimate, complete separation, and the total collapse of the soul's capacities to move, think, feel, hope, and trust. Although we can do nothing but admire St. John's perceptive and exhaustive treatment of the Dark Night, we must affirm that perhaps his understanding may be appropriate for monks of the Middle Ages whose entire vocation was to seek encounter with God resulting in union with Him. Ordinary Christian believers whose experience includes the diversions and hindrances of every day life do not reach that stage of paralysis of the ego's functions. But rather are given the grace of holding on to the hope of divine support and a sense of a continuing inflow of grace even in life's darkest moments.

We must expect to have experience of the dark and bitter times of spiritual blandness, which may reach crisis proportions. The undulation of the spiritual journey from the mountain tops to the dark valleys is well documented and an unavoidable pattern. But as the hymn puts it, "For

6. Second Corinthians 4:8–10.
7. Ibid., 4:16–18.

I know that whatever befalls me, Jesus does all things well,"[8] and we can count on the return of His restoring grace. The sunshine will appear again when the purpose of the dark is accomplished.

8. Fanny Crosby, "All the Way My Savior Leads Me," *The Baptist Hymnal*, 62.

35

Evenness of Spirit

THE APOSTLE PAUL SAID, "I know how to be abased and to abound. I have learned that in whatever state I am in, therein to be content."[1] He had achieved an "evenness of spirit" which produced an admirable sameness of state of mind regardless of the outward circumstances in which he found himself.

The Stoics valued "evenness of spirit" or "evenness of soul" as one of life's cardinal values, but they had scant resources for achieving this desired state of life. For them, the method was sheer determination to purge from the mind any disturbing conditions which would preclude serenity. Developing and maintaining an *apatheia*, a kind of detachment from all outward circumstances and an apathy toward distressing external circumstances, was their solution to the problem of achieving peace of mind. This method depended on a masterful exertion of will power and therefore was a function of the psyche, that is, a deliberate and intentional act of the soul without reliance on any transcendent sources or powers. As Epictetus, a leading Stoic philosopher, has famously said:

> True instruction is this:—to learn to wish that each thing should come to pass as it does. And how does it come to pass? As the Disposer, has disposed it. Now He has disposed that there should be summer and winter, and plenty and dearth, and vice and virtue, and all such opposites, for the harmony of the whole.[2]

Meister Eckhart ranks disinterest as the highest possible virtue and surest way to vital communion with God:

---

1. Phillippians 4:12, 11.

2. Epictetus, *The Golden Sayings of Epictetus XXVI*, trans. by Hastings Crossley, (Danbury CT: Grolier Enterprises Corp. 1980).

I have sought earnestly and with great diligence that good and high virtue by which man may draw closest to God and through which one may best approximate the idea God had of him before he was created . . . I find that [high virtue] to be pure disinterest, that is, detachment from creatures."[3]

Eckhart further states that, "You should . . . maintain the same mind, the same trust, the same earnestness toward God in all your doings. Believe me, if you keep this kind of evenness, nothing can separate you from God-consciousness."[4]

Evenness of spirit is an unmoving steadiness, a sameness, through all occasions, a consistency of mind that treats every situation as of equal importance or equally insignificant. It is being the same in every situation, maintaining a stayed mind, being unruffled, and unrattled regardless of the content of the moment.

Christians not only desire this state of evenness of spirit but have the assets for achieving it. These assets consist of their Lord and his salvation, His consolation and undergirding, and ultimately His indwelling in their own hearts. In short, the life of true faith is the only effective source for reaching the state of mind Paul refers to when he said that he was contented in any state of life in which he found himself in. "Not that I speak in respect of want: for I have learned, in whatever state I am, therewith to be content."[5]

Addison, the English essayist wrote on the condition we are calling evenness of spirit. Discussing the attitude of cheerfulness, Addison said:

I cannot but look upon it as a constant habitual gratitude to the great Author of nature. An inward cheerfulness is an implicit praise and thanksgiving to Providence under all its dispensations. It is a kind of acquiescence in the state wherein we are placed, and a secret approbation of the divine will in his conduct toward men.[6]

Isaiah wrote: "Thou wilt keep him in perfect peace, whose mind is stayed on thee: because he trusteth in thee."[7] To Isaiah, a mind "stayed" on God is the source of the evenness of "perfect peace."

---

3. Blakney, 82.

4. Ibid., 8.

5. Philippians 4:11.

6. Joseph Addison, "On cheerfulness," ed. Lindley Murray, *Sequel to the English Reader,* (New York: Printed and Sold By Collins & Co., 1818).

7. Isaiah 26:3.

Evenness of spirit is achieved not because every moment is reduced to nothingness, despair, blandness, which seems to characterize the Stoic way. Rather it is because every moment is elevated and seen to be of eternal value. Every moment of life is filled with divine content, containing an opportunity and invitation for us to perform the will of God. This gives us the privilege of having no preference of one occasion over another. Every moment of the time of our life is God-filled. This allows us to have a high *apatheia*, that is to say, a sense that every moment is an exalted one containing just as much of God as any other. So we do not prefer one occasion over another. The *kairos* is not superior to the *chronos*. That one moment is more elevated than another is only a psychological state of our souls, not an objective quality of the superiority of one instant over another. All our times are in His hands and therefore all moments are equally filled.

The *apatheia* of the Stoics seemed depressed, melancholy, and bland. Such detachment indeed bespeaks an emptiness, coldness, and futility, devoid of emotional richness. But the high apathy of the Christian faith is rich and full. It is warm and fruitful. That every moment is equally valuable because it is equally filled with God's will, purpose, power, and calling, is liberating and inspirational.

After my original sojourn in paradise, I was better equipped to act on this reality—that every moment was charged with divine presence, and power and therefore in every occasion of life, whether full of human richness or a seemingly empty void, was in fact a gift from God which contained His full will, presence and power.

Of course, this serenity of soul that Paul referred to is achievable through the consistent practice of the Christian faith. It is not necessary to have been taken up into paradise to gain this evenness of spirit. The general dynamics of Christian practice, which we have delineated as drawing near to the Christ who dwells within every believer's heart and referring all our cares and concerns to Him, are sufficient to achieve this excellent condition of soul. In my own case, I found that this quality was greatly enhanced in me after my transcendent experience, which I have described as "being taken up into paradise." But this and all Christian virtues are attainable by practicing Christians and does not require exalted religious experience.

36

The Still Small Voice

AFTER HAVING BEEN WITH Him in paradise, we find new inner conversation going on within us. The still small voice becomes more
distinct and forceful. So many spiritual values are not available to us until
we have been taken up to glory and committed ourselves wholly to Christ.
Among these is the "still small voice."[1] It would be tragic and disastrous
for us to try to follow the still small voice within us before we have made
the commitment and have successfully practiced radical obedience for a
time. This is because the inner voice may be nothing more than that of our
own conscience, a function of our own psyche. This inner dialogue may
be nothing more than a conversation with ourselves. But after we have
achieved some degree of this kind of commitment, the still small voice is
purged of the purely human element and reinvested with the voice of God
and therefore becomes the word of God to us.

We cannot follow the still small voice absolutely in the beginning
because of the distortions of our own self-centeredness. Sin has transformed it into our own voice, the voice of conscience, which is variable
and subjective. The inner voice given in and with our creation has been
distorted by the attachment of our own desires, hopes, dreams, intentions, understandings, interpretations to it and our control over it. So we
cannot, in the beginning expect to be able to follow it absolutely; totally
disregarding common sense, reason, expectations of family and society.
The still small voice is distorted by our own selfish will, our own sinful
desires, our attempts, subtle and unrecognized, to make it say what we
want it to say.

We expect the still small voice to say what supports success, happiness, and our own sense of well-being, normalcy, that which is approved

---

1. First Kings 19:12.

by the culture of the times and the community expectation. Of course we cannot turn ourselves over to this voice under these conditions. The divine element is crowded out and subdued.

When we have achieved a higher degree of faith, the still small voice becomes clear, distinct and is harmonized with the true interests of the soul. Then it will have been purged of the imputation of our desires, wishes, wants, hopes and dreams. Its clarity and authority are restored. When we radically follow Jesus, the voice becomes clear, vital, forceful, authentic and absolutely trustworthy. Then we can obey it categorically without qualification to the total disregard of our own understanding, will, desires and the desire to control the outcome of our lives.

A contemporary assumption is that if we follow Christ, we will be a "success." This is a fatal expectation, devastating to our spiritual lives. It starves our souls, distorts our spirits and sentences us to confusion, frustration, dissatisfaction and alienation. We must therefore surrender everything to Jesus. Then, after sufficient practice of radical obedience, the still small voice will become what it truly is—the voice of God. Then we can then follow it absolutely and without qualification. Then we can activate the scriptural injunction to "Trust in the Lord with all thine heart; and lean not unto thine own understanding."[2] We know that our understanding is the product of the spirit of the Lord. It is a divine gift. For as Job says, "But there is a spirit in man: and the inspiration of the Almighty giveth them understanding."[3] But as we have seen, we have distorted this divine gift, made it a vehicle for our own desires and therefore reduced its power and authenticity.

The challenge to "lean not to your own understanding" is a call to restore the genuineness and divine authority to the inner voice by purging it of all our own interests, including our spiritual interests. We must sacrifice even our own spiritual interests; we must surrender concern for our own souls for Jesus if we are to obey Him radically. Just as He sacrificed Himself absolutely and ultimately for us, we must sacrifice ourselves absolutely and ultimately for Him. Perhaps in any given crisis in which we find ourselves He will rescue us at the last moment. Or perhaps He will not. We must af-

2. Proverbs 3:5.
3. Job 32:8.

firm our commitment in the same words He used, ". . . nevertheless, not as I will, but as thou *wilt.*"[4]

Only by making ourselves a living sacrifice can we restore this voice as the voice of God. Then ". . . my God shall supply all your need according to his riches in glory by Christ Jesus."[5] Then He will give heavenly gifts. Spiritual values and eternal treasures will flood the soul.

4. Matthew 26:39c.
5. Philippians 4:19.

37

Seeing Everything *Sub Specie Aeternitatis*

AFTER WE ENTER INTO vital communion with God in the sacred room, everything in the world looks very different. We see things from God's point of view; we grasp everything under the aspect of eternity. The philosopher Spinoza[1] used this term *sub specie aeternitatis* to indicate a certain way of looking at reality. Seeing things from God's point of view would produce a totally different understanding. In Spinoza's case, if one saw things *sub specie aeternitatis,* one would see reality as one thing, having one substance, and in fact see that everything is God and God is everything. Although we are borrowing Spinoza's phrase, we do not accept his radical monism as a metaphysical position. But it is a convenient way of viewing our subject. In fact, after being with Christ in paradise, everything *does* look different.

After we begin experiencing Him deeply and powerfully from within, then we see Him everywhere from without. Just as wearing sun-glasses gives a certain shade of color to everything we look at through them, the spiritual glasses we acquire in the sacred room impose the vision of Christ upon all reality.

Without this kind of inwardness, all our professed visions of Christ have a certain artificiality, a pronounced vacantness. But with it we can see Him everywhere and in everything. After being with Christ in paradise, such thought no longer seems strange and overdrawn. But rather, after we have thoroughly embraced Him within the sacred room and beheld Him with an inner seeing, we are given a new outward seeing that perceives Him everywhere and in everything.

---

1. Spinoza *Ethic* Prop. XLIV pt 2, John Wild, ed.,(New York: Charles Scribner's Sons, 1930).

This comprehensive vision must grow out of the inner beholding of Him or it is contrived and barren, not to mention, very pantheistic. Dwelling in the sacred room with God reveals the truth that every common bush is aflame with His presence, and that His glory is as pronounced in the shop and at the hearth as it is in the cathedral and stained-glassed sanctuary. We are as greatly lifted up by the wind rustling the grass as we are by the peals of a great pipe organ. The singing of a bird in the garden is as moving to us as the choir of hundreds singing Handel's "Hallelujah Chorus."

Coming to Him as He lives within the sacred room opens our outward vision to behold Him everywhere. How foolish and how naïve were the cosmonauts who, on returning from outer space proclaimed "We have searched the heavens and there is no God."[2] They could not find Him there because they had not found Him here. They could not come to Him in the heavens because they had not come to Him in their hearts. Yes, even in *their* sacred room He could have been found—for He dwelt in them even though they did not dwell in Him.

God always dwells in us but we are not always dwelling in Him. And how do we come to dwell with Him who is within us? Love is the way. The Apostle John says, ". . . he that dwelleth in love dwelleth in God, and God in him."[3] Even though God dwells in He soul of every person ontologically, every person does not dwell in God through faith in Christ. Love for God alone, expressed as faith in Christ, completes the circle and conducts us to God within our hearts, that is, within the sacred room.

2. Widely quoted in the media at the time.
3. First John 4:16.

38

The Opened Understanding

ONE OF THE BLESSINGS derived from our sojourn in paradise with Christ is an *opened understanding.* "Then opened he their understanding, that they might understand the scriptures."[1]

The natural understanding is a part of the ontological gift of God's breath which makes us human. The book of Job affirms that ". . . there is a spirit in man: and the inspiration of the Almighty giveth them understanding."[2] This level of our intellectual capacity is sufficient for application to the world in which we live. It is a valid capacity for all practical aspects of our lives. And although it is a part of the ontological gift of God that makes us human, the scripture indicates its limitations. "Lean not to your own understanding,"[3] we are told. "Commit all your ways to the Lord,"[4] the Bible urges. The implication is that if we commit all our ways to the Lord, then the Lord's understanding will become operative in our lives.

So we are challenged to replace the natural, human understanding with the divine. We exchange the ontological understanding with the wisdom of God through this option put before us. To lean on our natural understanding would be to rely on it, to trust it to a high degree, to consider it sufficient for every aspect of life. This exceeds its created capacity. If, therefore, we lean on God's understanding, it becomes operative in our experience and we have divine guidance.

In the Gospel of Luke, we find another dimension of heavenly aid to our faculty to understand. After Jesus' resurrection, He met some disciples

1. Luke 24:45.
2. Job 32:8.
3. Proverbs 3:5.
4. Ibid., 3:6.

on the Road to Emmaus. After convincing them that it was really Himself by showing them His hands and feet with their scars, Luke says that He performed the mighty act of opening their understanding. And this is related directly to the scriptures and is apparently an interpretative faculty which brings revelation to clarity. The mind of believers is opened to know the highest realities. The opened understanding is conversant with the divine mystery of the crucifixion and resurrection of Jesus. It is now equipped with a new faculty that would give access to knowledge which had been hidden. Until it was made the object of this imputed capacity to understand, it could be known as historical event or in a superficial way. The prophets and seers of the Old Testament spoke of God's partial and fragmentary disclosure of Himself but they did not know the full content of the divine secret, but now He ". . . hath in these last days (been) spoken unto us by his Son, whom he hath appointed heir of all things, by whom also he made the worlds."[5]

The opened understanding is apparently equivalent to the same reality about which the Apostle Paul wrote:

> Now we have received, not the spirit of the world, but the spirit which is of God; that we might know the things that are freely given to us of God. Which things also we speak, not in the words which man's wisdom teacheth, but which the Holy Ghost teacheth; comparing spiritual things with spiritual. But the natural man receiveth not the things of the Spirit of God; for they are foolishness unto him; neither can he know them, because they are spiritually discerned.[6]

The opened understanding referred to in Luke and the spiritual discernment of which the Apostle Paul speaks indicates a new way of knowing and lays down the concept of a spiritual epistemology. The natural understanding is to be put aside and not "leaned on" and replaced by the activation of the divine understanding, which now functions in the knowledge of a person. Then after Christ's resurrection, He performs an additional action by "opening" the understanding, specifically enabling it to grasp the meaning of the scripture. Paul interprets this further as being the capacity of spiritual discernment given in and with salvation, and thus unavailable to the "natural" man, that is, beyond the capacity of the ontological understanding.

5. Hebrews 1:1–2.
6. First Corinthians 2:12–14.

This new way of knowing, this spiritual epistemology opens realities to the believer which natural man cannot comprehend. Christ crucified no longer a stumbling block as it was to the Jews nor foolishness as it was to the Greeks but the power of God and the wisdom of God. Those who are called to saving faith have this new capacity to know, employing this spiritual epistemology. Those who have been taken up into paradise with Christ seem to have it more intensely.

But even so, we continue to falter and fall short of the will of God.

39

Gathering Experience for God

THE ONLY THING THAT is totally unique to us and therefore our ultimate irreplaceable contribution is our gathering experience for God. God wills to experience the world through me and again through every human person. This is what it means to be a human person: to be a gatherer of experience for God. He chooses to see the world through my eyes, to hear it through my ears, to touch it with my hands. This adds a dimension heretofore unavailable even to the Eternal One Himself and makes the divine life richer, fuller, adding to it the overplus of human experience.

The grief as I know it becomes His grief; the sorrow as I feel it becomes His sorrowfulness. God explores disappointment through my frustrations and set-backs. He goes with me into the surging upper reaches of joy when I traverse those happy dimensions. He laughs in my laughter, loves through my affection, shouts in my shout, feels exhilaration through my elevated emotions. Yes, He even wants to experience the cross of his own Son again with me as I have experienced it. To the darkness of the day when He turned His heart away from Calvary, He adds the light that lit my life when I stood before the broken form of the dying One to receive gifts beyond my highest joy.

So I say again, my purpose and yours and everyone's is to gather life for God, to collect experience for Him. This is the purpose beyond all purposes, the meaning undergirding all meanings, the reality which is the bedrock of all realities.

When I am searching for a reason to live, I remember this. God wants to live my experience with me. He wills to know historical life as I know it. My life therefore adds a dimension to God's. If I were not here in the world, God would be deprived of something of great value to Him—the stream of living experience that flows into His life through mine.

Although I may see no intrinsic value in my being here, God wishes me to collect experience for Him, to be His gatherer, selecting and living through the drama of life in both its commonplace and extraordinary dimensions.

God can hear the singing of the birds with His own "ears," but He wants to hear this music, which He Himself created, through my ears also. My ears and yours add a multi-dimensional stereophonic quality to the hearing of God, enhancing His own experience of the singing of birds. That is, our hearing provides an additional melody in a different key otherwise unavailable to Him. This melody contains the pathos and deep meaning inherent in the broken fragments of our human experience. When it falls on the appreciative "ears" of God, He rejoices to receive our contribution to His life and takes it into His own heart. God can smell the flowers with His own nostrils, but He wants to smell them through my nostrils too. Thus God's experience is further enriched through mine and yours.

God can see the crashing of the breakers on the ancient shore. He can behold the soaring mountain and see the starry heavens from the "other side," but He wills to see them through my eyes as He grounds my visual experience in His own being. In doing so, He makes His life richer and at the same time gives me a reason to be, providing me with a purpose for which to live.

When He bids me to gather grief, I know it is for Him, for His own use and purpose. When He wishes to collect joy and victory, He may send me or you out to get it for Him. In my hearing, He enjoys Beethovan's Fifth Symphony or Luther's hymn, *A Mighty Fortress is Our God*. Through my nostrils He smells the roses. In my tears He weeps. In my gathering of the fragments of life, twelve baskets full are left over for Him. In my experience He comes to know what even He, the Eternal One, could not otherwise know. Through the tattered bits and pieces of human lives, mine and yours, a dimension of existence is open to Him which even He could not create *ex nihilo*. The entire universe, the world and everything therein was created out of nothing at the Word of his mouth: "For he spake, and it was done; he commanded, and it stood fast."[1] But according to what He Himself has revealed to us, He must walk haltingly as I walk, weep passionately as I weep, laugh boisterously as I laugh, wait patiently

---

1. Psalm 33:9.

as I hesitate, heal slowly as I heal, and wound deeply as I am wounded. All of this is because He has chosen to live with me and in me, being a part of all that happens to me as I make my way through life.

In knowing that God is so related to me that He grounds all my experience in Himself, making it a part of His own inner life, then I, like the poet, Sarah Teasdale, ". . . snatched life back against my breast, and kissed it, scars and all."[2]

2. Quoted in Elizabeth Gray Vining, *The World in Tune* (New York: Harper & Bros., 1942), 31.

Bibliography

Addison, Joseph. "Cheerfulness." In *Sequel to the English Reader*, edited by Lindley Murray. New York: Collins & Co., 1818.

Anonymous. *The Cloud of Unknowing*. Translated by Evelyn Underhill. London: John M. Watson, 1950.

Anonymous. *A Guide to True Peace*. New York: Harper & Bros. n/d.

Augustine. *The Confessions of St. Augustine*. Translated by Edward B. Pusey. New York: Pocket Books, 1957

The Baptist Hymnal. Wesley L. Forbis, ed. Nashville: Convention Press, 1991.

Blakney, Raymond B. *Meister Eckhart: A Modern Translation*. New York: Harper& Row, 1941.

British Literature: Blake to the Present Day. Spencer, Hazelton, et al. Boston: D. C. Heath and Company, 1952.

Cassian, John. "Conferences." In *Nicene and Post-Nicene Fathers. Vol. xl*, edited by Schaff & Wace. Grand Rapids: Eerdmans, 1978.

Caussade, J. P. *Abandonment to Divine Providence*. Translated by John Beevers. Garden City, NY: Doubleday, 1975.

Chambers, Oswald. *My Utmost for His Highest*. New York: Dodd, Mead & Co., 1935.

De Sales, Francis. *Introduction to the Devout Life*. London: Burns, Oates and Washbourne, 1924.

Dionysius the Aeropagite. *Mystical Theology*. Wheaton, IL: CCEL

Edwards, Jonathan. "A Divine and Supernatural Light." In *Select Sermons of Jonathan Edwards*, Wheaton: Christian Classics Ethereal Library, 2000.

Finney, Charles G. *The Memoirs of Rev. Charles G. Finney*. New York: A. S. Barnes & Co., 1896.

Flammode, Paris. *The Mystic Healers*. New York: Stein & Day, 1974.

Guyon, Mme. *Experiencing the Depths of Jesus Christ*. Edited by Gene Edwards. (original title *A Very Short and Easy Method of Prayer*). Golenta, CA: Christian Books, 1975.

Hilton, Walter. "The Scale of Perfection." In *The Medieval Mystics of England*, edited by Eric College. New York: Charles Scribner's Sons, 1961.

John of Ruysbroeck. *The Adornment of the Spiritual Marriage*. Wheaton, IL: CCEL

Jones, Rufus M. *Some Exponents of Mystical Religion*. New York: Abingdon Press, 1930.

Kelley, Thomas R. *The Testament of Devotion*. New York: Harper & Row, 1941.

Kierkegaard, Soren. *Purity of Heart is to Will One Thing*. Glasgow: William Collins & Sons Co., 1938.

Law, William. *A Serious Call to a Devout and Holy Life*. Philadelphia: Westminster Press, 1955.

Lossky, Vladimir. *The Mystical Theology of the Eastern Church*. Crestwood, NY: St. Vladimir's Seminary Press, 1976.

McCutchan, Robert, ed. *The Methodist Hymnal*. New York: The Methodist Publishing House, 1939.

Mihajlow, Mihaljlo. "Mystical Experiences of the Labor Camps." In *Kontinent ii*. Garden City, NY: Anchor Press/Doubleday, 1977.

O'Brien, Elmer. *The Essential Plotinus*. New York: The New American Library, 1964.

Otto, Rudolf. *The Idea of the Holy*. Translated by John W. Harvey. New York: Oxford University Press 1958.

Page, Kirby. *Living Abundantly*. New York: Farrar & Rinehart, 1944.

Plato. *Phaedo*. Translated by Benjamin Jowett. Chicago: Encyclopedia Britannica, 1952.

Plotinus. *The Six Enneads*. Translated by Stephen MacKenna and B. S. Page. Chicago: Encyclopedia Britannica, 1952.

Plunket, Joseph. "I See His Blood Upon the Rose." In *Modern Religious Poems*, edited by Jacob Trapp. New York: Harper & Row, 1964.

Ruysbroek, Jan Van. *The Spiritual Espousals*. Translated by Eric Colledge. New York: Harper & Bros., n/d.

Schurmann, Reiner. *Meister Eckhart Mystic and Philosopher*. Bloomington: Indiana University Press, 1978.

Shakespeare, William. "The Tragedy of MacBeth." In *The Complete Works of William Shakespeare*, edited by William Aldis Wright. Garden City, NY: Garden City Books, 1936.

Spencer, Sydney. *Mysticism in World Religion*. South Brunswick New York: A. S. Barnes and Co., 1963.

Spinoza, Benedict Baruch. *Ethics*, edited by John Wild. New York: Charles Scribner's Sons 1930.

Strong, Augustus Hopkins. *Systematic Theology*. Philadelphia: The Judson Press, 1907.

Tauler, Johannes. *The Inner Way*. Wheaton: Christian Classics Ethereal Library (CD), 2000.

Thrasher, Kenneth L. *Jesus Christ Is With Us*. Smithfield, NC: Dayspring Press, 1983.

Theologia Germanica. Wheaton: Christian Classics Ethereal Library, 2000.

Teresa of Avila. *The Interior Castle*. Trans & ed E. Allison Peers. Garden City, NY: Image Books, 1961.

Vining, Elizabeth Gray. *The World in Tune*. New York: Harper & Bros., 1942.

Welch, John. *Spiritual Pilgrims*. New York: Paulist Press, 1982.

www.ingramcontent.com/pod-product-compliance
Lightning Source LLC
Chambersburg PA
CBHW060342100426
42812CB00003B/1097